A Separate Sisterhood

HISTORY OF SCHOOLS & SCHOOLING

Alan R. Sadovnik and Susan F. Semel
General Editors

Vol. 26

PETER LANG
New York • Washington, D.C./Baltimore • Bern
Frankfurt am Main • Berlin • Brussels • Vienna • Oxford

Katherine C. Reynolds
& Susan L. Schramm

A Separate Sisterhood

Women Who Shaped Southern Education in the Progressive Era

PETER LANG
New York • Washington, D.C./Baltimore • Bern
Frankfurt am Main • Berlin • Brussels • Vienna • Oxford

Library of Congress Cataloging-in-Publication Data

Reynolds, Katherine Chaddock.
A separate sisterhood: women who shaped southern education
in the progressive era / Katherine C. Reynolds, Susan L. Schramm.
p. cm. —(History of schools and schooling; vol. 26)
Includes bibliographical references (p.) and index.
1. Education—Southern States—History—19th century. 2. Education—
Southern States—History—20th century. 3. Women educators—Southern States—
Biography. 4. Educators—Southern States—Biography. 5. Southern States—Biography.
I. Schramm, Susan L. II. Title. III. History of schools and schooling; v. 26.
LA230.5.S6 R49 370'.82'0975—dc21 2002023805
ISBN 0-8204-5684-5
ISSN 1089-0678

Die Deutsche Bibliothek-CIP-Einheitsaufnahme

Reynolds, Katherine C.:
A separate sisterhood: women who shaped southern education
in the progressive era / Katherine C. Reynolds; Susan L. Schramm.
–New York; Washington, D.C./Baltimore; Bern;
Frankfurt am Main; Berlin; Brussels; Vienna; Oxford: Lang.
(History of schools and schooling; Vol. 26)
ISBN 0-8204-5684-5

Cover photo courtesy Museum of Education, University of South Carolina
Cover design by Lisa Dillon

Contents

Illustrations

Preface

We undertook this study with little more than a realization that many impressive women had left enduring marks on various aspects of southern education during the early decades of the twentieth century. Just as a school child learns to attach the names of U.S. states to their capital cities, we had learned through reading and research the names and matching accomplishments of these educators—Cora Wilson Stewart and the Kentucky "moonlight schools" for adult literacy; Annie Webb Blanton and the Texas State Superintendency of Education; Mary McLeod Bethune and Bethune-Cookman College for African American youth; Alice Lloyd and a college to produce leaders in Appalachia; Wil Lou Gray and the "opportunity schools" that led South Carolina to the first state-supported adult education; as well as dozens of others responsible for institutions, policies, and practices that would enhance educational opportunities in the South.

We found ourselves questioning why, given recognition of their names and accomplishments, these women had never been situated as a collective force or viewed as a distinct subgroup within a larger context. We sensed that their individual contributions took on smaller historical importance than they deserved because they occurred in separate and scattered spheres that had not been conceptualized or understood with a view toward commonalities and coherence. Although they were of the Progressive Era, they had not been perceived in standard terms of club work, social activism, or progressive educational pedagogies. Although they were of the South, their experiences, racial mix, and socioeconomic backgrounds ranged too widely to define a collective heritage from southern lady to new woman. Although they were women, feminist interpretations of agency and oppression did not fully explain their complex motivations and sometimes anti-feminist tactics.

To a very large degree, the southern circumstance, with its scattered rural population, its wide-ranging racial and class mix, and its uncertain economic bases, kept educational accomplishments dispersed and seemingly unrelated. As Joseph Kett noted of southern women in humanitarian, "socially progressive" causes, women working in education undertook different routes to reform than their northern counterparts because "advocacy of education in the South was less specialized, less tied to the narrow disciplines being spawned by schools of pedagogy in the North." Two important factors noted by Kett combined to relegate southern women to educational reform work that developed individually and in relative isolation: (1) the need for rural outreach in their work and (2) their lack of "either specialized pedagogical training or easy access to state educational administrative agencies."[1]

Still, we intuitively agreed with the notion of studying and understanding a group of women as a whole, as Penina Migdal Glazer and Miriam Slater had so convincingly managed with their 1987 study of women in medicine, academe, and social work, *Unequal Colleagues: The Entrance of Women into the Professions, 1890—1940.* We recognized that accomplished Progressive Era women in education, like their counterparts in other professions, were marked for their pioneering roles by what Glazer and Slater noted as "a belief that they could forge a synthesis between the Progressive sense of burgeoning opportunities and the separate, more constricted world of female endeavor."[2]

Our study began with a question and a quest. First, we asked about the experiences, influences, aims, successes, and failures of the many women of accomplishment in southern education from approximately 1890 to 1930. We understood the forces following the Civil War that drew many women from the safety of upper-class home-making and plantation management to teaching as a suitable way to meet new middle-class economic realities. Other women of the Reconstruction Era—mostly missionaries from the north or African Americans with a year or two of normal schooling—turned to teaching when schools backed by churches and missionary societies offered the only educational opportunities for the children of newly freed slaves. But we wanted to discover the somewhat later forces that guided pioneering women educators who moved beyond teaching to become crusaders, founders, administrators, and policymakers during a time when the South had barely begun to grudgingly accept a public persona for women.

Second, we wanted to present what we found in a way that would encourage an understanding of these southern women as a collective entity—a separate sisterhood constructed of very different individuals who stood together metaphorically to shape important southern educational advances during the Progressive Era.

We selected biographical approaches for our work for reasons similar to those noted by Anne Firor Scott in her 1984 collection *Making the Invisible Woman Visible.* "Life histories," Scott insisted, "contribute to that imaginative feel for the past without which even the most careful accumulation of data is sometimes lifeless." Further, she noted, life narratives are particularly appropriate for southern histories because they are consistent with the southern penchant for story telling.[3] Our own approach was to examine a large number of women who shaped southern educational reforms in the Progressive Era, to watch for categories in which they might be grouped, and to select several women in each category for further biographical research. Thus, our study is not a comprehensive history, but a grouping of exemplary women whose lives and works are examined as a way of uncovering influences, motivations, aims, and contributions of women who worked separately but with a shared commitment to advancing southern education.

The multifaceted women selected for our research seemed eligible for any number of arrangements and groupings that might frame their various endeavors and organize their life experiences into some discrete categories. For purposes of this study, we selected a framework that emphasizes their primary arenas of accomplishment in education. Although almost all the women we studied made important contributions in more than one arena, the educational reform work for which they were known enabled us to view them as:

(1) Collegians (who emphasized reform as expanded general academic and social opportunity through preparatory and collegiate institutions);
(2) Vocationalists (who emphasized reform as enhanced economic opportunity through education for employability); and
(3) Systems thinkers (who emphasized reform as improved policies and practices that spread their influence throughout state or regional systems).

Such categories themselves may indicate some of the shape of Progressive Era educational reform efforts in the South, as well as the differences evidenced in northern and southern progressive endeavors. For example, women in the North and Midwest who initiated educational strides during the same period gained particular prominence with regard to enlarging opportunities for urban immigrants and founding schools along the lines of John Dewey's concepts of progressive education. Several notable women, such as Celeste Parrish and Marietta Johnson, also initiated child centered institutions in the South. These schools and their founders, however, are more appropriately studied in the context of progressive educational philosophies than that of southern regional particularities.

Nearly three decades after the publication of her groundbreaking book, *The Southern Lady: From Pedestal to Politics, 1830—1930,* Anne Firor Scott noted that her 1970 work was just a step ahead of "what would become an avalanche of work on the subject" that indicated new directions among historians, especially female historians.[4] Our work in researching and writing *A Separate Sisterhood* has benefited from many of the studies that might be viewed as part of that avalanche, including historical accounts of conditions in the South, feminist interpretations of women's struggles for identity and agency, analyses of educational reforms during the Progressive Era, and examinations of women's entry into roles as activists and professionals.

Particularly informative have been several analytical texts that offer interesting interpretations of gender and regional questions. For example, Joseph F. Kett, in "Women and the Progressive Impulse in Southern Education," observed that "social progressivism" was the aim of both northern and southern women who "sought to ameliorate social conditions without fundamentally altering the distribution of political and economic power among classes."[5] Yet, Kett recognized substantial regional differences in the means by which southern women could tackle progressive causes, generally occasioned by lingering traditions that located them as homebound ladies and by their need to sidestep racial issues in order to garner extensive support of powerful white elites.

In another study dealing with gender issues during the Progressive Era, *Pedagogies of Resistance,* Margaret Smith Crocco, Petra Munro, and Kathleen Weiler tackled the history of educational reform from a gendered perspective. Viewing educational attainment and education careers as empowering forces for women, the authors traced the means by which women were able to engineer social change in a highly gendered world. Additionally, they challenge many historical interpretations they perceived to "have separated, too rigidly in our view, the child-centered from the social-reconstructionist form of progressive education."[6] Similarly, Sari Biklen reported in *School Work: Gender and the Cultural Construction of Teaching* that teaching created a forum to inspire nineteenth century female activism.[7]

In *The Power of Femininity in the New South,* Anastatia Sims observed that, at least for those women not constrained by race or class, involvement in socially progressive clubs and organized advocacy groups paved the way for empowerment outside the home and a growing sense of professional competence. Many women used their new-found power to push for better school facilities, more inclusive curriculums, compulsory attendance laws, and longer school years.[8] Another route to southern women's empowerment—higher education—was traced by Amy Thompson McCandless in *The Past in the Present: Women's Higher Education in the Twentieth Century American South.* McCandless studied not only the female institutions, from finishing academies to normal schools and excellent colleges, but also the forces that guided the distinct education of a southern woman and the ways in which those forces influenced the curricula of southern colleges well into the twentieth century.[9]

A number of informative studies in recent years have examined the struggles of women entering various areas of professional employment. Although they do not specifically tackle leadership in southern education, they demonstrate that women attempting to carve a significant place for themselves outside the home confronted similar contexts. Robyn Muncy, for example, demonstrated the paradox of autonomous control circumscribed by traditional expectations of female behavior in *Creating a Female Dominion in American Reform, 1890--1935.* Observing women in social work, public health nursing, and home economics, she found that when women's work was limited to service and to women's issues, gender politics had little effect; however, when women accumulated policymaking power in these areas, gender issues again moved to the forefront.[10] Covering the same time period, Glazer and Slater traced the uphill battles of women entering the traditionally male spheres of medicine, science, and academic scholarship; Hawks and Ellis recounted women's attempts to campaign their way into elected state offices; and Anne Goodwyn Jones offered evidence of the struggles and achievements of southern women writers.[11]

The studies of southern women and their entry into spheres outside the home that joined the "avalanche" touched off by Anne Firor Scott's earlier work are both particularized and contextualized by a number of edited volumes that have collected essays and reports of specialized historical studies. Those offering diverse and in-depth glimpses into any number of issues concerning gender, class, and race among southern women are: *Taking Off the White Gloves,* a 1998 study edited by Michele Gillespie and Catherine Clinton that features southern women on southern history; *Hidden Histories of Women in the New South,* a 1994 collection of little know victories for women in various parts of the region edited by Virginia Bernhard et al.; Anne Firor Scott's own collection of her essays and lectures concerning the history of southern women, *Making the Invisible Woman Visible;* a 1991 collection of feminist issues and success stories edited by Noralee Frankel and Nancy S. Dye, *Gender, Class, Race, and Reform in the Progressive Era;* and *The Web of Southern Social Relations,* edited by Walter J. Fraser, Jr., et al., and published in 1985 to illuminate the ways in which family, education, and women contributed to the social fabric of the South before and after the Civil War.

By locating women at the forefront of educational reform in the South during the Progressive Era, we intend to add new perspectives to the growing body of literature on various aspects of southern womanhood and southern education. Importantly, we aim to honor the work of women educators as a "group" that carried on separate reform efforts and innovations while establishing a sisterhood of feminine influence.

Acknowledgments

Our research and writing would not have been possible without the assistance of librarians and archivists who are the key agents of access to primary data. We particularly thank the excellent staff members at the United States Library of Congress; the North Carolina State Division of Archives and History; the Arthur and Elizabeth Schlesinger Library, Radcliffe College; the Southern History Collection, University of North Carolina at Chapel Hill; the South Caroliniana Library and the Museum of Education, University of South Carolina; the Center for American History, University of Texas at Austin; the McGaw Library, Alice Lloyd College; the Library and Archives, Bethune-Cookman College; and the Martha Berry Museum, Berry College.

Among the colleagues and friends who provided support and assistance, we especially thank Dr. Dennis Carlson, Miami University; Ms. Catherine Monrad, Brown University; Mr. Brett Reynolds, University of Chicago; and Dr. Dan Ruff, Ms. Karan Romaine, Ms. Tammie Powell, and Ms. Mary Grimes, University of South Carolina. Most importantly, we are grateful for the encouragement and patience of our families when we most needed it.

CHAPTER ONE

Southern Realities as Context for Reform

When educational reforms during the Progressive Era (approximately 1890 to 1930 for purposes of this study) are located in the domain of noteworthy curricular and pedagogical changes, the southern states* generally are found outside the geographic parameters of advanced professional practices and experimentation. Yet, as several scholars have suggested, educational advancements of the Progressive Era were not typified only by the readily identifiable and highly publicized activities of the Midwest and Northeast and were not restricted to coherent philosophies and goals of a well-defined "Progressive Movement."[1]

In his classic episodic history, *The Transformation of the School* (1962), Lawrence Cremin tried valiantly to salvage the notion of "progressive education" with the recognition that the concept could not be defined, but the insistence that it did have various elements of shared meaning among its proponents. However, his thorough and detailed discussions did not attempt to account for

* This study concerns itself with the states of: Alabama, Arkansas, Florida, Georgia, Kentucky, Louisiana, Mississippi, North Carolina, South Carolina, Tennessee, Texas, Virginia, and West Virginia.

different and complex proponent motivations, such as social control versus social service.[2] Nor did Cremin, or many other analysts of progressivism in education, attempt to explore in any detail the possibilities of regional differences in educational reforms that occurred during the Progressive Era, possibly because many regionally specific endeavors fell outside even the most loose approximations of the "progressive education" label.

Peter Filene has charged that "a diffuse progressive 'era' may have occurred, but a progressive 'movement' did not." He concluded that progressives acted in "shifting coalitions" rather than a single movement and noted the possibility of regional groupings of progressives. However, he saw too little philosophical consistency within regions to consider identifying their shared nuances.[3] When Herbert M. Kliebard determined that progressive educators might have found at least some common ground in "reform subgroups," he described those groups as having like ideologies, a construction that could fit some regional groupings but not others.[4]

While these scholars may have sensed regional issues at play in the Progressive Era, they found more evidence of regional diversity than of geographically specific convergence around collective goals and beliefs. However, Jeffrey E. Mirel cautioned that geographical distinctions could not be ignored among the variables that shaped varieties of responses to educational needs. Assumptions about the exemplary nature of Midwest and Northeast educational reforms and about the existence of a definable movement, according to Mirel, "distort our understanding of this crucial era because both glibly assume uniformity and consistency in two areas marked by enormous diversity and change—educational politics and policy, on the one hand, and local and regional history, on the other."[5]

The American South was, as these analysts intimated about all geographical regions, a place of widely ranging educational ideals and objectives during the Progressive Era. Yet, the southern region was marked by distinctive historical, social, and economic realities that certainly influenced the nature of its responses and adaptations to various brands of social, political and educational progressivism experienced throughout the country. The venerable and highly regarded interpreter of the region, Wilbur J. Cash, writing late in the Progressive Era, noted in the southern states "a fairly definite mental pattern, associated with a fairly definite social pattern," and maintained that "the peculiar history of the South has so greatly modified it from the general American norm that, when viewed as a whole, it decisively justifies the notion that the country is not quite a nation within a nation, but the next thing to it."[6]

Edgar W. Knight also found in the South a separateness formed by unique circumstances that combined with national conditions to guide twentieth-century educational activities of the area: "Extraordinary economic and political conditions and forces have had tremendous influence on the development of secondary education for both whites and Negroes in the South," he insisted. "And the difficulties which have faced secondary education in the Southern States can be understood only in light of the conditions and forces at work in that section."[7]

The unique southern context set complex, often contradictory, forces into play when reform sentiment spread to venues below the Mason and Dixon line. William Link found that Progressive Era "reform" values clashed with local "traditional" values in a paradox that framed the actions and outcomes of the southern reform endeavors. While paternalistic reformers saw social problems ripe for contemporary practices toward improvement, traditionalists found comfort in the heritage of tight communities united in antigovernment sentiment. Reformers, confronting inadequate social, political, and educational conditions in rural and poor areas "offered uplift and improvement, but wanted to limit local participation and control. They eventually discovered that their success depended on the cooperation of communities that more often than not were reluctant to sacrifice neighborhood control."[8]

Typical of many Progressive Era endeavors throughout the country, southern educational reforms, whether inspired by local agreement or paternalistic reform measures, often were more opportunistic than intentional. They occurred within a context of symbiotic combinations of local and reform sentiment that owed much to fortunate timing and the presence of determined individuals. Undergirding them was a shared sense that the South was a distinctive culture whose members suffered together in the humiliation of the Civil War and subsequent economic disaster. These realities offer a backdrop for tracing in the South some patterns and groupings of Progressive Era reform activities that were distinct from one another in ideology and method but were connected by contextual circumstances fairly unique to their region.

Economics and Isolation

Any account of education in the South during at least a century following the Civil War cannot underestimate the contextual starting point of devastating societal and political defeat, extreme poverty, rural isolation, and widespread illiteracy. Prompted by such realities, early twentieth-century southern journalist Gerald W. Johnson reminded, "We cannot forget the pit whence we were digged, nor the crushing toil that went into the digging. What went on in the South between 1870 and 1900 was too completely tragic to furnish the material for theatrical tragedy…."[9]

Edgar Knight maintained that educational events in the South could only be accurately measured against a southern starting point, rather than in comparison to the rest of the country. While he warned against "historical alibis" in explaining why southern education, for the most part, lagged behind the rest of the country by mid-twentieth century, he insisted, "Those lags, on which much has been written, have chief explanation in the past and especially in the economic, political, and social past of that section of the United States designated by the satirical pen of Mr. Mencken as the 'Sahara of the Bozart'."[10]

By the dawn of the Progressive Era, at the close of the nineteenth century, little basis existed for instilling new curricular and pedagogical concepts in a region where 25 percent of those working in cotton mills were well under 16 years old, the average school term was 93 days (shorter still for African American students), the taxable wealth backing each child was one-fifth the amount available in the North and West, and only one southern state (Kentucky) had passed compulsory education legislation. These were common patterns in the South at a time when educators in the North pondered how, not whether, learning would take place among the next generation of the region's citizens. According to Tulane University scholar Stuart G. Noble, "Economic retardation is largely responsible for the backwardness of [southern] white as well as negro schools."[11]

Joseph Kett, who found the rural and dispersed southern population to be an even greater impediment to educational advancement than the region's extreme poverty, emphasized significant regional differences in the contexts confronted by progressives. "Southern Progressives had to swim in a different ocean, to confront a radically different society than the one northern Progressives lived in."[12]

After the devastation of the Civil War and the freeing of slaves for whom education had previously been illegal, statistics about the South easily portrayed a backward region that would be slow to catch up with other regions even as industrialization promised new financial possibilities. Illiteracy was widespread among southern citizens 10 years and over at the turn of the century, amounting to 48 percent among African Americans and 12 percent among whites. Chipping away at the need to educate disenfranchised black citizens, Freedmen's Bureau teachers and denominational mission schools helped to close the gap over time. By 1920, 26 percent of the South's black citizens were considered illiterate, compared to 6 percent of whites.[13]

Even while Wilbur J. Cash lauded the South's "mighty development of the passion for education" at the end of the first decade of the twentieth century, he admitted, "The standard, to be sure, was still pathetically low. The rural school was ordinarily a one-room shack and ran only three to five months in the year.

And the teachers, grotesquely ill paid, were literate only by the most elementary measure."[14] Although urban blight was the target of many progressive social reformers in the North, the rural and dispersed population of the South presented perhaps even greater challenges. In 1900, 84 percent of southern citizens lived in settlements of fewer than 2,500. The only cities of over 100,000 in the region were Memphis, Louisville, and New Orleans.[15] In a report submitted at the Fourth Conference for Education in the South, in 1901, G.S. Dickerman noted that the 10 southernmost states, with a combined area 85 times as great as Massachusetts, had only 19 cities with over 25,000 inhabitants, compared to 10 cities that size in Massachusetts alone. The consequences, Dickerman noted, were "superior schools in the larger centers, with none to match them in the rural districts. A fine thing for the centers but ruinous to the hamlet."[16]

The South of the late nineteenth and early twentieth centuries offered far shorter public school years than those provided in the North, as well as fewer total grade years. While the average days of school attendance per child each year exceeded 100 days in 17 states in the North and West, the number sank to 47 in Alabama and was no more than 72 in any southern state. By this measurement, the South fell below an unimpressive national average of just over 80 school days a year, a situation that was shocking enough to prompt the Russell Sage Foundation statement, "As a nation the United States has a shorter school day, a shorter school week, and a shorter school year than any other highly civilized country in the world."[17]

Child labor undoubtedly colluded with inadequate educational financing to limit school years and average student attendance. In 1900, one-fourth of all cotton mill operatives throughout the South, and nearly one-third in Alabama, were under 16 years old; and thousands of those were under 14.[18] In Louisiana, Nevada, Texas, Alabama, Virginia, and South Carolina, more than one third of children of school age were not enrolled in either public or private schools in 1910. Especially for African American students, southern schools offered very short school days and years.

Again, the Russell Sage Foundation candidly recognized the consequences: "It is evident that Vermont, Maine, and Connecticut, with more than 90 percent of the children of school age actually in school, are making better investments in future citizenship than Alabama, Texas, and Louisiana." [19] In Atlanta, in 1913, double sessions in black schools meant that 5,000 students were in school only three hours a day.[20]

Low school attendance and short school years in the South were matched by excessive under-spending. In 1902, Atlanta, New Orleans, and Memphis schools spent, respectively, $1.90, $1.74, and $1.61 per pupil. Yet, in the same year, the average for all cities over 25,000 was $4.37 per pupil.[21] Regional differences in annual expenditures could not be explained by the shorter school years in the South according to a 1910 survey. Whereas average expenditure per child per day was more than 20 cents in most states of the Northeast, Midwest, and West, it ranged in the South from 7 cents in North Carolina, South Carolina, and Georgia to 15 cents in West Virginia and Louisiana.[22]

Teachers, like other wage earners in the South, were paid well below those in the rest of the country. By 1910, average annual public school teacher salaries ranged from $200 in North Carolina to $384 in Texas. The nationwide average was $485, with a high of $918 in California.[23] Robert A. Margo used U.S. Bureau of Census data and adjusted daily wages to length of school year to develop 1910 wage figures for white and black public school teachers in the South. The discrepancies included $694 annually for white teachers in South Carolina, compared to $251 for black teachers, and $640 annually for white teachers in Louisiana, compared to $240 for black teachers. By 1936, the earnings gaps had narrowed only slightly: Black public school teachers in Mississippi were paid less than one-third the earnings of their white counterparts; and black public school teachers in Florida, South Carolina, Louisiana, and Alabama were paid less than one-half the salaries of their white counterparts. As the authors of the 1910 Russell Sage Foundation study reported about the southern states, "In some of them domestic service pays better than teaching school."[24]

Ironically, the South's large proportion of citizens under 20 years of age made improved education both more necessary and less likely than elsewhere. By 1930, more than 50 percent of the residents of South Carolina and nearly 50 percent of those in North Carolina were under 20 years old. Nationally, citizens under 20 comprised less than 40 percent of the population.[25] During the second decade of the twentieth century, the southern states had 1,279 school age children for every 1,000 adult males, compared to 789 per 1,000 in the northern states.[26] According to North Carolina journalist Gerald W. Johnson, these profiles meant, "The Southeast has proportionately more children to feed and educate, and fewer adults in the prime of life to do it than any other region. It follows that in this region we should expect to encounter the greatest difficulties in the elimination of child labor and in the provision of the best type of public education—which is exactly what we do find."[27]

Even the most optimistic analysts of the southern endeavors during the Progressive Era found scant evidence of educational progress. Arthur S. Link became one of the first to pronounce reform success in the region, when he applauded the presence from 1880 to 1920 of a "a far-reaching progressive movement in the South."[28] However, even Link's heady sense of an identifiable "movement" was limited to findings about farming, politics, journalism, and railroad transportation. Education was not among his examples. Further, he admitted, "As far as progressive democracy went in the South, it was progressive democracy for the white man."[29]

The Southern Way of Being

Southern poverty and rural isolation were important influences on education before and during the Progressive Era, but these also were joined by southern attitudes and political interests in fully shaping the nature of educational progress. Perhaps most striking was the intersection of racial prejudice with educational and economic aspirations, conditions that led Stuart G. Noble to succinctly conclude, "If schools for white children are poor, the schools for negroes are poorer."[30]

The leading edge of the Progressive Era found the South circling the wagons of racism with sham responses to "separate but equal," with legalized disenfranchisement of African American citizens, and with political control of schools and school systems by white elites. It quickly appeared that any immediate reforms in the region likely would be paternalistic accommodations contributing to a program of change that C. Vann Woodward eventually characterized as "progressive for whites only."[31]

Disenfranchisement for the black population spread readily to education throughout the Progressive Era, "disinheriting the Negro educationally," according to David Tyack. By 1932, Tyack noted, differential treatment was so extreme that one county in South Carolina spent $8 on each black student in public schools while spending $178 for each white student. Replete with lopsided reform efforts and white elitism, southern education clearly reflected the widespread racist sentiment of the region and called into question the existence of any genuinely progressive ideals in the South. In some instances, as when enhancements for white schools were funded by reducing or closing black schools, educational reform appeared more regressive than progressive. William A. Link eventually concluded that "school reform—in more obvious ways than other varieties of reform—exposed a fatal flaw in Southern Progressivism."[32]

Robert Margo found that per pupil expenditures in southern public schools were relatively similar for black and white students late in the nineteenth century, but began to shift toward much lower expenditures for African Americans around the turn of the century. The gap grew and persisted until moves toward equalization in some areas in the 1940s.

Two explanations posed by Margo for the widening gap in school spending by race were the loss of political clout, even before formal disenfranchisement, and shift of funds away from black schools to meet reformers' demands for better white schools.

By the turn of the century, Democrats had returned state governments to the white elites, where necessary by election fraud. Local appointments from the state level assured white supremacy in expenditures at all levels; and poll taxes, literacy tests, and the like denied blacks the ballot. It is possible that only the need for some small nod, albeit in name only, to the legal requirement of separate but equal kept many public schools for African Americans open at all. Margo notes that philanthropic funding from entities like the Anna T. Jeanes Foundation and the Julius Rosenwald Foundation also shared some of the credit for the survival of African American education in the face of unfavorable southern economic circumstances and elite white political control.[33]

Racism and economic elitism combined to motivate southern whites to seek for African American students just enough schooling to become literate and just enough industrial training to become the instruments of capital seeking cheap labor. Many white elites, as well as northern philanthropists, found they could support the idea of educating black students to stay in their places as trained cooks, porters, tobacco workers, farm operatives, and lumber mill hands. Poor whites, for the most part, cornered the semi-skilled and unskilled jobs in the textile industry, while elite whites filled the white collar arena. Black citizens could be trained to work harder and faster at the remaining laboring jobs, but perhaps not so well trained that they could readily leave the farm or factory. Industrial training also met with approval from those whites who doubted the cultural maturity of the African American race.

However, as James D. Anderson reported in his study of 75 years of black education in the South, the talk about manual and industrial training for southern blacks did not translate into widespread efforts in that direction. "Concentrating largely on the political and social implications of an educated black laboring class, many white southern politicians and school superintendents often made no significant distinctions between black industrial and academic schooling."[34]

The Hampton and Tuskegee programs of semi-skilled occupational training and manual labor as disciplinary education were controversial among many black citizens and did not provide as much strictly industrial training as many whites would have preferred. Furthermore, some whites were concerned that even industrial training could raise the economic level of black citizens who might then become a political force or might leave the rural South. Apparently, there was at least scattered sentiment that impoverished black schools, with their short school years and offerings of little above the elementary level, were preferable to training that might lead to greater economic independence among African Americans in the South.[35]

Mission societies, generally elements of various denominational aid efforts initiated in the North, were responsible for the majority of available African American education that approximated college preparation or college-level learning in the early twentieth century. Their private schooling helped to fill the gap left by separate, but certainly not equal, federally funded land grant colleges for black students. Mission successes included colleges such as Fisk, Morehouse, Clark, Claflin, Bennett, Benedict, Allen, Spelman Seminary, and Stillman Seminary. For the most part, such efforts reflected a desire to train black leaders; and, as Anderson suggested, "To these philanthropists, black leadership training meant, above all, higher classical liberal education."[36]

Thus, among many denominational missionary efforts toward educational reform, intellectual attainment and liberal culture were more prominent objectives than vocational placement.

Northern industrial philanthropists were more disposed to the vocational training model of education for blacks, and during the Progressive Era they managed to increase white support for this concept as well as for compulsory education laws and other policies toward more widespread, if agenda-laden, public education (Anderson, 1988). However, industrial training was hardly a new idea in the South or exclusive to black citizens, although it was an attractive notion for the schooling of marginalized groups. In 1885, Mississippi established an Industrial Institute and College for Girls; and in 1896, the Alabama Girls Industrial School opened—both promoting useful skills in homemaking and secretarial venues for white females. Additionally, the push for manual and agricultural training, as well as domestic science courses, was taken up for white public schools during the first two decades of the twentieth century, with those in Georgia, South Carolina, Virginia, and North Carolina experiencing state legislation that called for at least some types and levels of public school vocational training. With the passage in 1917 of the Smith-Hughes Act, federal funding for vocational training prompted the expansion of occupational education in the curriculum of secondary schools throughout all regions, including the South.[37]

Regardless of varying educational philosophies and disagreements about objectives and means, there was little opportunity for the secondary or post-secondary schooling of southern blacks in the early twentieth century, including badly needed teacher training, outside privately funded institutions. In a particularly dark period in its history, the U.S. Supreme Court in 1899 ruled in *Cumming v. School Board of Richmond County, Georgia* that the Augusta, GA, board of education had not acted unconstitutionally when it closed the only public high school for African Americans in the county, Ware High School, in order to divert savings to black elementary schools. Regardless of the separate but equal doctrine established three years earlier in *Plessy v. Ferguson,* Justice John Marshall Harlan's majority opinion side-stepped that principle in favor of his rationalization that the school board would close both black and white high schools if it did not prevail and that the plaintiffs needed to demonstrate that racial hostility was the sole motivating factor in closing the high school.

By 1915, there were no public high schools for blacks in 23 southern cities of 20,000 or more inhabitants, although those cities together had 36 public high schools for white students. Even in the cities where black high school age citizens outnumbered white high school age citizens (e.g., Montgomery, Savannah, Shreveport, Wilmington, Charleston, Jacksonville, Jackson, and Vicksburg), the public high schools were available only to whites. In 1914, the board of education of Atlanta reduced the public grammar school course of study for blacks from eight years to seven years; in 1916, the board decided to abolish the seventh grade for blacks and replace it with industrial training. Where black public schools did exist, their conditions often were deplorable. For example, in 1912--13, the average class size in southern public schools for blacks was 67.[38]

To a greater extent than the dispersed rural citizens, black urban dwellers should have been able to use proximity to their advantage to protest and politic against the extremes of discrimination demonstrated in their schools. It is a testimony to the stranglehold of white elites on all governmental systems that such protests were long ineffective. David N. Plank concluded, Blacks, teachers, and other constituents of the school system sometimes stirred up public debate over educational issues, but they were never able to threaten the political control of the elite or the commitment of city governments to "sound business principles" and low taxes. As a result, improvements in the quality and quantity of educational opportunities in southern cities came slowly, when they came at all, and southern school systems continued to lag behind those in northern cities.[39]

Active and powerful political forces were not the only element working against the advancement of education and other opportunities for southern blacks. Gerald Johnson noted that there was little agreement among southerners about any need to attend to racial issues at all. What critics considered a race problem, many southerners saw as no such thing. Inequities were the natural way of maintaining fragile economic and social balances. Johnson's example characterized a northern critic stating the problem as, "In the South the negroes are a dominated race; how can we release them?" Yet, he viewed the southern understanding of the issue as, "In the South the dominated race are negroes; how dare we release them?"[40]

In keeping with Johnson's observations of blinding historical and social legacies, as well as pre-formed southern white opinion, Jack Temple Kirby argued that black disenfranchisement was itself the great progressive achievement for reform-minded southerners. He explained, "So far as most whites were concerned, counting out Negroes politically and socially made possible nearly every other reform they might undertake—from building better schools to closing the saloons."[41] The South, apparently, spawned responses to reform needs that often were unique to its situation and uniquely unsuited to the spirit of progressivism. Any educational advancements of the era that embraced the democratic ideal of progressivism needed to occur as niche reforms-individual and local efforts scattered about as models and examples, rather than widespread commitments with the force of political and public support.

Reform from a Different Starting Point

To what extent did the distinctiveness of the southern conditions and attitudes produce distinctive educational reforms during the Progressive Era? In other words, could the widespread national impulse for political and social reform find similar expression in the educational arenas of the South as it did in other regions?

The answers to these questions can vary, largely depending on how inclusively, or perhaps even vaguely, we define the notion of "reforms during the Progressive Era." Confining the definition to particular sets of curricular and pedagogical practices leads to the conclusion that transformations sought by adherents to a progressive education "movement" were not as plentiful in the South as elsewhere. Additionally, as George S. Counts pointed out to the discomfort of many, the progressive education movement was highly exclusive toward the educational lives of middle-class children surrounded by people "who are full of good will and humane sentiment, who have vague aspirations for world peace and human brotherhood." To be "genuinely progressive," according to Counts, such a "movement" would need to extend to all children, "face squarely and courageously every social issue, come to grips with life in all of its stark reality, establish an organic relation with the community, develop a comprehensive theory of welfare...."[42] Clearly, this was not the case in any single region, but even less so in the South.

However, social adjustments (whether toward service or control) that could impact educational change through more efficient and professional governance and through increased citizen inclusion did occur with varying degrees of speed and success in many parts of the South. Typically, these were not the top-down products of the influential "administrative progressives" identified by David Tyack. Nor were they often rooted in the work of educational developmental theorists and practitioners. Instead, southern reforms frequently were consistent with Jeffrey E. Mirel's conclusion that many important reforms happened not top down, but bottom up. Interest groups that played significant roles in educational reform of the era, but have had only limited recognition, according to Mirel, include women's organizations, organized labor, and ethnic groups.[43]

Social progressives in the South (and those from the North who spent time and/or money in the South) joined under a big tent and sometimes hit upon educational reform agendas almost by accident. When they campaigned for literacy, voice in government, child labor restrictions, agricultural extension, suffrage, or social welfare, they were advocating educational reforms at some level. Others started with educational reform as a route to dealing with other social and economic issues—especially those African Americans who saw the need to establish private schools and colleges as a way to overcome the limited provisions for public schooling for blacks. Some scattered efforts even tested progressive curricular and pedagogical practices in schools modeled on patterns gleaned from John Dewey and William Heard Kilpatrick.

For Dewey Grantham and other South watchers tinged with optimistic good will, the dawning of a New South at the start of the twentieth century meant economic growth and progressive ideals. Such observers pointed to roots of southern progressivism in a mistrust of big business interests, a growing white middle class, civic clubs, child welfare concerns, and political campaigns that included in their rhetoric the uplift of the common man. Grantham referred to the South's "great educational awakening soon after the turn of the century." However, he noted that where educational reform did exist, it fit C. Vann Woodward's description of a "mixture of paternalism and noblesse oblige which is the nearest Southern equivalent of Northern humanitarianism."[44]

While the South made some headway in the availability and professionalization of public schooling in the early decades of the twentieth century, even an optimistic Grantham recognized that "Most white southerners shared in the consensus...that blacks should be kept in a subordinate position. Many southern progressives were willing to use racist means in their efforts to accomplish political and social reforms, and even the minority of whites that criticized repressive measures against Negroes were often motivated by a concern for whites rather than blacks."[45]

To some extent, school reform in urban areas experienced common expressions in the North and the South, especially in terms of changes in school board election methods and increased advocacy for higher teacher pay.[46] However, the students attending urban southern schools were disproportionately white. Few to no high schools existed for black citizens early in the twentieth century in the southern cities, and far shorter academic programs were available to them. Thus, comparisons from South to North in this area may emphasize disproportionately the effects of reform on white students.

Racial inequities, fueled by deep white resentment and fear after Reconstruction, sparked the establishment of private black schools by denominational missionaries, freedmen's societies, and various grassroots efforts supported by local donations and northern benefactors. Progressive era reforms for black students needed to aim at enhancing the quality and quantity of such schools, as well as advocating the sharing of public school opportunities with white students. For example, black schooling in Atlanta started in a church basement just after the Civil War and continued in a discarded railroad car commandeered by the

American Missionary Association. The endeavor to privately educate African Americans grew painfully slowly and could not keep up with need, even with inroads such as Morehouse College and a number of well-regarded and academically oriented private secondary schools.[47] With northern philanthropy moving toward industrial training, the black population was sorely limited in gaining a foothold in academic advancement on par with the white population. In 1940, only 16 percent of Georgia's black 15 to 19-year-olds were enrolled in public schools, and only 1.7 percent of the cohort graduated from public high schools.[48] While the Progressive Era witnessed increased black political clout that broadened the base of inclusion in public schooling, clearly much remained to be done.

Social reform appeared to have the upper hand over child-centered progressive impulses in the South, making the spread to educational reforms somewhat random and opportunistic. There was far less professionalism and disciplinary specific emphasis in either social work or education among southern reformers than among their northern counterparts, a factor that Joseph F. Kett found at least partially responsible for the entry and persistence of many women in the southern reform arena. Although these women were active together in a variety of broad-based clubs, especially in urban areas, they did not network extensively along professional lines.[49]

Southern educational reformers also were separated in terms of southern differences generated by prevailing attitudes of individualism and localism. Many mill families, for example, resented the push for more strict child labor laws. Their long established family and economic patterns depended on child labor, and they viewed threats to it as threats to their family structure.[50] The paradox that pitted strong sentiment for local control and tradition against new practices transferred from other regions resulted in a patchwork of reform efforts that changed substantially according to local need and individual influence. And, as already indicated, issues of race and rural isolation separated southern reformers and reform agendas still further.

Oddly, perhaps incredibly, educational reforms did find southern venues during the Progressive Era. However, those reforms are best evidenced in specific and anecdotal efforts driven by the commitment and energies of forceful individuals. Their work could not be easily located in one place or in one method of practice and instead surfaced as a collection of varied and far flung endeavors, diverse in philosophical direction and often experimental in intention. Rather than adhering to new professional ideals sparked by William James, John Dewey, and others, educational "progressivism" in the South took multiple directions toward new institutions, newly served populations, policy and systems changes, and other reforming endeavors. And, like much about the South, early twentieth-century progressivism was intensely personal in design and substantially influenced by the experiences and personalities of individuals who forged new paths in education and elsewhere.[51]

The educational reforms of the Progressive Era in the South, therefore, may be even further from a "progressive movement" than Filene found in "shifting coalitions" that formed and reformed around various issues and aims.[52] Southern reforms were widespread, anecdotal, and not always issue oriented. They often started at the point of the solution (e.g., fund adult night schools; start a college; raise teacher pay), with only limited data about the underlying issue or its natural constituency. Southern educational reformers were often improvisational and intuitional, frequently working single-handedly until small groups of supporters gathered. Many of them were women.

CHAPTER TWO

Down from the Pedestal: Women in the Progressive Era South

Enlarging the body of literature on southern Progressive Era reform requires disclosing the motives, perspectives, achievements, and processes of southern women educators who worked in the former Confederacy with its history of slavery and traditions of white male supremacy. Since these women were expected to defer to men, their battles against an exclusively male educational establishment to win social justice through better schools, better working conditions, and better salaries were all the more complex. Often they used their collective strength to fight the men who held positions of power over them. Moreover, with the South in the grip of Jim Crow, some of the women defiantly worked with black colleagues, joining their struggle to secure racial equality in public school education.

Often women who were not committed to racial hierarchy and gender stratification and who dared to question the status of women, working-class poor people, and people of color were considered radical—a perception that partially explains their exclusion from social and economic histories. But more significantly, as Simone de Beauvoir observed in *The Second Sex*, women seemed locked out of transcendence not by being female but by the *meaning* attached to being female.[1]

Anne Firor Scott, Anastatia Sims, Jean Friedman, and Dewey Grantham established that the South had its own unique brand of Progressivism and that southern women were vigorous advocates of such humanitarian causes as education, settlement houses, the abolition of child labor, better schools, and public health.[2] Many middle-and upper-class women in the South focused their attention on what Joseph Kett termed "social Progressivism," emphasizing issues traditionally identified with the domestic sphere—children, the family, the poor, and the neighborhood.[3] According to Kett, "social Progressivism" provided them with a "spacious theater for their reformist activities"[4]

Unpacking the narratives of the personal and professional pasts of southern women educators who worked in a society joined to the twin idols of patriarchy and white supremacy reveals authentic accounts of the problems and struggles they encountered. We situate their efforts within the context of southern gender perceptions and realities in order not to homogenize away local differences and local controls but to celebrate the regional differences.

Sometimes labeled radical within the context of their time and place, these women often defied custom by assuming left-leaning political stances. Their commitments to women, blacks, and labor often marked them as subversive, un-southern, even un-American in the minds of conservative antagonists. Their struggles to secure equal rights for women, blacks, and poor whites and their insistence upon academic freedom and economic justice may have aroused opposition; but they also often garnered impressive support at the grassroots level and among civic leaders, academics, and political figures. Their careers and their accomplishments present a valuable reminder that not all southerners shared the values of southern traditionalism.

Remnants of the Victorian South

Following the Civil War, southern women were faced with the paradoxical situation of dealing with Victorian Era ideals and sanctions while exploring the new educational and vocational opportunities that characterized the dawn of the modern era. To illustrate, the traditional doctrine of spheres—the private and the public—posited a clear separation between the domestic and the political worlds. The separation of work roles in modern industrialized American society relegated women to the home, and the "cult of domesticity" emerged as a direct response to modernization.[5]

The problems of combining family and career were logistical as well as ideological, as the time and energy demands of working both inside and outside the home were formidable. It is not surprising, therefore, that most of the women in this study never married and a few separated or were divorced. The problems of career and family were a continuous struggle for women seeking both personal and professional fulfillment.

In her quintessential book, *The Southern Lady: From Pedestal to Politics, 1830–1930,* Anne Firor Scott portrayed the significant role actively played in the political arena by southern women during the Progressive Era.[6] Scott confessed that before going North to college and leaving her native Georgia for the first time, she believed in the authenticity of the fabled antebellum image of the "southern lady." "Like the fish who has to be landed to perceive water, I became seriously aware of southern history only at Harvard, away from the South."[7] Many women struggled to free themselves from cultural expectations, and Scott described the realities of women's lives which were often at odds with the "lady" image. In the South, the social role of women was "unusually confining" and the sanctions used to enforce obedience "peculiarly effective."[8]

Scott explored the intersection of race and social class, observing that the role expectations for women of color and working-class poor white women varied from women of educated and wealthy families. "When they sweated in the fields or tore their hands digging in the ground no one lectured them on feminine delicacy or told them it was unladylike to work so long and hard."[9] For the most part, it was the southern women of educated and wealthy families who came out of the domestic circle to work, live, and act in a broader society and leave their mark on the historical and public record. In the 1995 revised edition of *Southern Lady* Scott included an afterword, "The Southern Lady Revisited," in which she described the primary drawback of the original 1970 edition as her failure to incorporate the perspectives, patterns, and attitudes of black women.[10]

The lives of southern women—both black and white—are shaped by a peculiar regional heritage that sets them apart from their sisters elsewhere. Southern women, regardless of color, ethnicity or social class, shared aspects of strength and oppression and developed strong coping mechanisms to deal with the demands of an insensitive patriarchal society. Although many of these women clearly struggled with the patriarchal bureaucratic systems they encountered and sometimes challenged, by and large, their unprecedented achievements in the public sphere during the Progressive Era were gained not by reconceptualizing institutionalized sexist, racist, and classist practices, but by thinking and acting within the constructs of those realities in ways that were socially acceptable. Women's clubs and benevolent organizations were viewed as particularly appropriate avenues for women who joined the reform impulse. The field of education offered respectability, and there were few other respectable paid occupations for women in the nineteenth and early twentieth centuries. In addition, education suited the ideological motives of women who considered their careers in education a form of religious, social, or political activism.[11]

Constructions of gender that deemed women pious, pure, submissive, and domestic produced the ideological glue that held southern middle-class white culture together. The "cult of true womanhood" acknowledged women to be naturally spiritual and motivated only by an unselfish concern for others.[12] Middle-class white Americans had, in the nineteenth-century, invented a set of prescriptions for female behavior and assumptions about women's nature that largely excluded women from the public spheres of politics and business. According to Robyn

Muncy, the "cult of true womanhood" is a belief system that "proclaimed women the natural harbors of spiritual and moral values in the wildly acquisitive seas of Jacksonian America and further apotheosized women as that half of the human race motivated only by concern of others."[13] In all she did, woman was to sacrifice individual ambition in order to serve; and she served best through childbearing, charitable activities, teaching, and nursing.[14]

Although southern white women managed to slowly venture into the workplace, the market, and the polity, the needs of families and children both framed and limited the public domain for them. Entreating their maternal duties to protect children and care for the poor, many women organized around local issues: the improvement of working conditions, especially for women and child wage earners; maternal and child welfare; clean water; pure food and milk; adequate sanitation; improved housing; and, most importantly, schooling.

The Feminization of Teaching

By the mid-nineteenth century, girls' chances to attend grammar school or what is known today as high school—not to mention university—were slight. The "female academies," attended mainly by daughters of the upper classes, were not numerous, and they varied in their emphases, often stressing social or domestic subjects. However, by 1890, more girls than boys were graduating from high school and high school attendance gave women access to better jobs, notably in school teaching.[15]

The feminization of teaching took place in the nineteenth and early twentieth centuries because of three simultaneous and interdependent developments—(1) the popular acceptance of teaching as a critical and acceptable "female" occupation; (2) the opening of normal schools and other higher education institutions to women; and (3) the economic need to staff the new tax-supported common schools with large numbers of inexpensive teachers.

After the Civil War, there was a surplus of women especially in the South because so many young men had been injured and killed. Although immigration eradicated much of the surplus, especially after 1880, many southern women sought jobs. It is therefore probable that with the loss of so many men of marriageable age during the Civil War, southern women sought alternative opportunities to support themselves.

Moreover, the crucial need for schoolteachers, at first visible in the antebellum decades, became even more pressing after the Civil War on several counts. Northern women with an evangelical missionary spirit flocked to the South where they found a new focus in educating the men and women recently freed from slavery. They especially felt that the desolate rural areas, heavily populated with working-class poor people—both white and black—desperately required their services.

The forced reevaluation of society that accompanied the end of slavery logically extended to a reconsideration of the status of southern women, and reconstruction generated hope for the educational advancement of women and blacks. At the end of the Civil War, many of the "good" families in the South found themselves either impoverished or financially bound to a relatively humble level of existence. Economic necessity following the war was largely responsible for many young women of good family name to seek employment as teachers since teaching had long been considered an honorable occupation for this socioeconomic group. School teaching continued to provide women with important ways to serve society and support themselves, and it was postbellum daughters of all backgrounds that needed to support themselves or assist their struggling families that swelled the ranks of women teachers.

Economic necessity also fueled a drive for advanced education, resulting in the expansion of normal schools for teacher training. The founding in 1884 of the exclusively white Mississippi State Normal and Industrial School initiated a pattern soon followed by Georgia, North Carolina, South Carolina, Oklahoma, and Texas. These institutions provided a briefer and less expensive course of study for teachers than that of colleges.[16]

Until 1850, men had dominated the teaching profession, but as economic opportunities increased in industry, trade, and other professions, they took better paying jobs and left teaching to women.[17] Women schoolteachers, like women in other fields, were paid far less than men. In the 1820s, for example, a woman teacher earned around twenty dollars a school session, while a man teacher earned one hundred dollars.[18] By the 1840s, women teachers were paid about a third as much as were men, and the gap never narrowed throughout the century. Teaching was never a high status profession in the United States, and by the end of the nineteenth century, it unfortunately sank even lower in prestige as it became dominated by women.[19]

Despite significant strides in educational and occupational advancement, prejudice and discrimination against working women continued to prevail. Once women began to enter male-designated occupations, those fields lost their professional status. Women teachers and nurses, for instance, received less pay for the same work that men did; and the more profitable professions remained dominated by men. By the Progressive Era, as school populations and budgets soared, male-controlled school bureaucracies designed for "efficiency" curtailed the autonomy of the classroom teacher.[20] The most influential Texas women educator of the early twentieth century was Annie Webb Blanton, elected state superintendent of public instruction in 1918 and a longtime professor at the University of Texas.[21] Blanton's contributions to the teaching profession included the improvement of the working conditions and the status of women. Believing that the potential of feminine leadership was unlimited, she argued that merit not gender should determine leadership roles in education. She founded Delta Kappa Gamma in 1929 and continued to nurture and strengthen the organization until her death in 1945.[22]

Because women were thought to be naturally more religious, more caring, and more virtuous than men, they felt they had a special social, moral, and educational mission. An essentialist view of gender holds that women are biologically predisposed to particular feelings and behaviors such as caring, compassion, and service. This view also holds that it is necessary for women to be subordinate to men. Essentialist arguments assign certain proclivities to the genders—men are responsible for the head, and women are responsible for the heart. Women instruct young children because they are emotional and fragile, and men supervise women and children because they are analytical and sensible. Thus, it was thought of as "natural" within the evolution of bureaucratic school systems that men should manage and that women should teach.

The new tax-supported common schools needed large numbers of inexpensive (therefore, female) teachers, and increasing numbers of women needed a source of income.[23] In Lotus Coffman's 1911 study of teachers, he argues that the increasing number of women in the teaching force was:

> Due in part to the changed character of the management of the public schools, to the specialization of labor within the school, to the narrowing of the intellectual range or versatility required of teachers, and to the willingness of women to work for less than men . . .all of the graded school positions have been preempted by women; men still survive in public school work as "managing" or executive officers.[24]

By the mid-nineteenth century, economics as well as essentialist ideology supported the emergence of careers for women in education, and nearly two-thirds of all the teachers in the nation's schools were female.[25]

During the Progressive Era many school buildings in the South were dilapidated and dirty, especially in the rural areas.[26] Schoolrooms were often sparsely furnished and lacked blackboards, maps, and other basic equipment. They were poorly lit, inadequately ventilated, and cold in winter. Poor sanitation made schools breeding grounds for disease. Students often drank from a common dipper in a water bucket and used open outdoor latrines, and provisions for the disposal of trash and human waste were inadequate.[27] Reformers found in the dismal state of southern rural school facilities an explanation for the high rates of illiteracy and truancy. They recognized that the drab surroundings made learning difficult. "In the present condition of the average school house it is impossible to train the youth of the State properly" Elvira Moffitt of North Carolina complained.[28] Improving school facilities was the first step in upgrading the educational system. And who better to supervise the cleaning, decorating, repairing, and landscaping of schools than the same people who performed those tasks for their husbands and children?

Higher Education Opportunities for Women

By the mid 1800s, middle-class white women used the "cult of true womanhood" to justify their admission to higher education.[29] They argued that if they were to be the best possible mothers and wives, they needed the finest educations. The first women's colleges opened in the South.[30] In 1836, the Wesleyan Female College of Macon, Georgia, became the first educational institution in the country to award higher degrees to women. Judson College, a similar institution, was founded in Alabama in 1838, and the Mary Sharp College for women, now extinct, was established in Tennessee in 1852.[31] By 1870, one-third of American colleges and universities admitted both women and men; by 1890, two-thirds did; and before the turn of the century, women accounted for 36 percent of America's undergraduates and 13 percent of its graduate students.[32] By 1900, the number of coeducational colleges and universities reached 71.6 percent.[33]

From the onset of the Civil War to World War I, three critical forces contributed to women's advance into higher education. First, was the popular trend in public education, evident in the growth of common schools and high schools. Second was the more immediate impact of the Civil War and Reconstruction which initiated new opportunities for women as a group, both in employment and in education.[34] Third, the ferment and expansion in university education included strides in women's education, even though skepticism lingered about the value of higher education for women.[35]

A variety of collegiate institutions grew in religiously, socially, and racially heterogeneous America. Between the 1850s and the 1870s several models developed: (1) the private women's college; (2) the religiously oriented coeducational college; (3) the coordinate women's college; (4) the secular coeducational institution, both public and private; and (5) the single sex vocational institution.[36] Before the Civil War fewer than six American colleges adopted coeducation, but by 1870, 29 percent of universities were coeducational in the United States.[37] As people pushed westward, beyond the Mississippi, every state university, except that of Missouri, was coeducational from its beginning[38]—probably more because of financial reasons than for reasons of social justice. The East moved more cautiously; Cornell University was the first eastern public school to become coeducational, in 1872.[39]

Throughout the nineteenth-century South, however, single sex institutions of higher education remained the norm for white women. It was not until the early twentieth century that all state universities admitted white women in the South, with the exception of three—the University of Georgia, the University of Virginia, and Louisiana State.[40] Ironically, Atlanta University, the first coeducational institution of higher learning in the South, was founded by the Congregationalists for African Americans.

Women's ability to function as educators at the turn of the twentieth century depended, as it had earlier, on their own access to higher education. Some feared that higher education would raise women above the duties of her position as wife and mother. Feminists such as Lucinda H. Stone and Sarah Dix Hamlin made vigorous attempts to defend higher education for women.[41] They argued that women were not intellectually inferior to men and their admission in large number would not make it impossible to create true universities in America as some alleged.[42]

Despite a deep-seated skepticism on the part of the public with respect to the value of higher education for women by the late nineteenth and early twentieth centuries, many women focused their energies on higher education as a means toward other improvements in women's status and in society. In 1920, although the male-controlled campuses were often hostile, there were reasons to see a promising future for women in the field of education. The percentage of women among college students had risen from 21 percent in 1870 to 47.3 percent, and women were a quarter of college faculty and 86 percent of classroom teachers.[43] Still women were a small minority of the growing numbers of educational administrators at all levels, and in higher education women students and faculty were ghettoized in the less prestigious and remunerative fields. Although a serious backlash to women's progress in many areas of public life, including education existed, women gained ground as a significant portion of the working population especially in schools.

Diversity Among Southern Women Educators

Like the much larger population of women educators from whom they are drawn, the educators profiled in this volume came from different social and ethnic backgrounds. Most were white, but some were African American. Some had access to travel and elite colleges and universities, while others struggled to acquire higher education at small religious institutions, normal schools, or public universities. Their ideological and political endeavors, including their views on women's roles, ranged from ultraconservative to radical liberal.

For the southern daughters from middle class backgrounds, social feminism often took root among those who typically made a commitment to socially useful work after graduating from college. These civic-minded women had the ability to draw people to their causes. Their varied approaches to those causes depended, in part, on precedents established by the strong southern families from which they came. Sarah Towles Reed's stable family background, for example, contributed to her self-esteem, which enabled her to confront local authorities in New Orleans on controversial issues of teachers' associations and unions. According to Leslie Gale Parr, "Although Reed had no aristocratic pretensions, she possessed the self confidence that came with membership in a respected family with deep roots in the antebellum South."[44]

For the African American educators, race was usually more salient than gender, although many also found voice in feminist causes. For instance, Nannie Burroughs saw her career as a contribution to the uplifting of women in the African American community; and Mary McLeod Bethune founded a school for African American girls and directed its development into a coeducational college. Bethune also played a leadership role in several national women's organizations, lectured, wrote newspaper columns, and advised President Franklin Roosevelt's administration on matters concerning youth, education, and African Americans.[45]

By the late nineteenth century, southern women—both black and white—working toward social justice had developed a strong sense of community involvement, working as volunteers in myriad organizations and as paid employees in business and education.[46] They often advanced to positions of leadership within the organizations they created and were successful at building networks that gave them political influence.

At the same time, opposition to women's suffrage, education for women, and the transition of women into the public sphere often came from women themselves. The Gramscian theory of hegemony illustrates this phenomenon since hegemony, widely defined, is the process whereby a dominant group constructs its ways of seeing social reality so successfully that its views are accepted as normal and commonsensical, even by those who are in fact oppressed or disempowered by it.[47] William Link described the comments of one North Carolina woman who was vehemently opposed to challenging traditional gender roles.

> Southern women did not like to "mingle in politics." Rather they preferred to leave "the men to manage the government their own way, . . . feeling glad to be free from a responsibility" at interfered with more congenial duties. Women were "not made that way" and cared little about exercising their 'talents in such a manner.[48]

A female passing comfortably from private to public sphere was viewed as a threat to southern chivalry and custom. Not surprisingly, many women backed away from activities they feared violated a system of gender relations they viewed as secure. With women in the political sphere, the social equilibrium would be destroyed and chaos would follow since by "unsexing" themselves women would undermine domesticity and maternity norms. The formation of these views can be traced to the evangelical community of the Old South where women were encouraged to invest all of their emotional, productive, and social energies into spouse, family, and household.[49]

However, from the beginning of industrialization in the early nineteenth century, women were a significant portion of the working population. In the manufacture of textiles, one of the first major industries, women workers often outnumbered men.

In the South in 1807, for example, 3,500 women and children worked in 87 cotton mills and outnumbered men by seven to one.[50] However, these women and children earned less than their male counterparts for comparable hours doing the same work. An 18-hour workday with a wage of $1.50 a week was not unusual, even at a time when people needed at least $10.00 a week to meet basic expenses.[51]

The notion of progress seemed especially adaptable to the American situation, including women's situations, in the late nineteenth and early twentieth centuries given the wealth of opportunity in the new land. As people continually pushed westward toward the frontier, the idea of progress coincided nicely with the conviction of manifest destiny. An optimistic atmosphere was created by talk of democratic government and the idea that responsibility for the quality of life lay in the hands of the people. Educational institutions and educational systems became obvious items of interest for those who wanted to hasten and enhance progress and work toward social justice.

To more fully understand the individual biographies and collective contributions of southern women educational reformers working during the Progressive Era it is useful to consider their commitment to social reconstruction and programs for the development of citizenship and responsibility. One of the characteristics of the modern era is *the hope of progress*. As educational historians such as Herbart Kliebard; Daniel Tanner and Laurel Tanner; and Joel Spring have shown, early twentieth-century America was characterized by social meliorism—the idea that the world tends to get better and that this tendency could be furthered by human efforts such as improving people's health, living conditions, and education.[52] Almost universally accepted in the modern era was the idea that *progress* would lead to the future perfectibility of human beings. Coupled with their firm embrace of family and community, this concept was particularly appealing to women. They could then readily fit into this modernist notion of "progress" the perception of schooling as a vehicle for improving the human condition. This dominant ideology was a crucial motivator for many women who devoted their lives to disseminating education among marginalized groups that they believed, in turn, would lead to the betterment of the whole society.

In retrospect, the modernist idea that humankind advances and continues to move in an improving direction is viewed by postmodern theorists as one of the most important myths in education.[53] Moreover, early progressive pedagogy is characterized as conservative in intent and outcome by postmodern theorists because it did not acknowledge race, class, gender, and sexuality as involved in organizing our culture in profound and far-reaching ways.[54] For example, Dewey's seminal text, *Democracy and Education*, a study of pedagogical principles and practices in a democracy, attacked the pedigreed alliance between culture and social class that was reflected in unequal access to school curriculum (as well as in the curriculum itself), but did not specifically address issues of race, gender, or sexuality.[55]

Regardless of today's contemporary critiques on early Progressive Era education, the concept of progress is still a very powerful and persuasive ideal in American culture. Because they believed that the improvability of people is inherent in schooling, the reform discourses of the women discussed in this book are organized around stories of progress. And it is through this lens that we re-construct the lives of these distinguished yet historically silenced and invisible southern women school reformers of the Progressive Era who struggled for social justice.

Collegians, Vocationalists, and Systems Thinkers

The experiences and actions of the southern women educators discussed in this volume sometimes intersect or overlap. However for the purposes of this study the women are categorized as:

(1) vocationalists (women whose work emphasized employability through vocational skills);

(2) collegians (women who created opportunities for collegiate and/or college preparatory education); and

(3) systems thinkers (women who worked to reform educational policies and practices through broad social and political systems). While the discussion of each area notes the contributions of many notable women, several are treated with biographical detail that studies their influences, motivations, struggles, and achievements.

Charlotte Hawkins Brown, Alice Lloyd, and Martha Berry are categorized in this study as a "collegians" because they were concerned with extending pre-collegiate and collegiate level general and liberal education to those whose opportunities had previously been circumscribed by race or gender discrimination, economic circumstances, and/or geographical isolation. They saw general and liberal education at the postsecondary level as a way to build qualities of leadership and character, to support regional and racial uplift, and to open a range of professional career opportunities.

Nannie Helen Burroughs, Mary McLeod Bethune, and Elizabeth Evelyn Wright are described as "vocationalists" because they were concerned with the seemingly immediate economic uplift that education could provide for those who would otherwise have no marketable skills. Their goal was to give students the ability to achieve and retain economic stability by providing them not only with necessary skills but also with the cultural capital required for success in the American capitalist system such as punctuality, proper grammar, and writing proficiency. They targeted blacks and women who had few good jobs open to them. In retrospect, they appear to have accommodated elite white preferences for an unskilled, but eager, labor force among southern blacks. However, their very short-term focus on the immediate and local needs of the poorest of the poor may demonstrate more astute pragmatism than political naiveté.

Finally, Cora Wilson Stewart, Wil Lou Gray, and Annie Webb Blanton are distinguished as "systems thinkers" since they perceived widespread governmental influences and activities as the key to educational reform. They were natural networkers who operated within the confines of large bureaucratic systems to build coalitions among diverse groups in order to bring reform and innovation to large numbers of southerners. Although they neither consciously attempted to reconfigure the fixed order of bureaucracies nor challenge the patriarchal status quo, their efforts within established channels did shape new educational programs and policies. For example, when these women were working in the field of education, the National Education Association was dominated by male administrators, with the (mostly female) teachers subordinated and largely silenced within the association's leadership. Although, male-dominated structures may not have been lost on the systems thinkers, their energies were spent less on challenging that reality and more on improving the human condition through education.

Many southern women during the Progressive Era sought to reform education; and through their histories, their thoughts, their philosophies, and their creations we can find ways to understand their past achievements and their collective influence for our contemporary purposes. The concerns of the women in this study dovetail with those of Progressive Era reformers in the North and throughout the United States. They frequently stood in the forefront of social activism, occupying a minority position and seeking to rally others to their cause. Their stories attest to a long tradition of civic activism among southern women and constitute an important chapter in the ongoing story of southern liberals' efforts to transform elements of their society from within.

CHAPTER THREE

Collegians: Liberal Learning and Higher Education

Not unexpectedly, the women who focused reform efforts on southern postsecondary education and college preparatory studies typically were those who themselves had at least some higher education or reason to appreciate the value of higher education in the early twentieth century. The "collegians" of this study are those women whose educational perspectives were imbedded in personal familiarity with cultural and intellectual preparation that could provide both the social and mental refinements long viewed as the fruits of higher education—especially liberal education. They understood that the historic deficiencies of southern education left a need for both preparation for work and preparation for life, and quite often a need for remedial work prior to that preparation. Those whose work led them to develop new higher education programs and institutions did so only after at least some effort to put secondary, pre-collegiate programs on solid footing.

Importantly, however, these women brought healthy doses of traditionalism to their reform efforts. The educational "reforms" they sought might be better characterized as "realignments" which would not mark radical change in the substance or methods of education, but would represent steady progress in increased access to many types of education and increased opportunity for furthering learning beyond the high school level. The most successful of such endeavors appropriately recognized the southern citizens' discomfort with notions that might threaten their affection for community, tradition, family, and religion. Women who initiated educational strides in the South during the Progressive Era were able to work within these realities, often because of their own grounding in southern traditionalism.[1]

While working toward increased opportunities for higher education among southern students, often aiming their endeavors at African Americans or rural whites, these women rarely entered directly into the fray of the Booker T. Washington v. W.E.B. Du Bois debates which were simplistically characterized as questions of vocational training or liberal education. Both choices were deemed necessary by reformers attempting to create postsecondary options for people with a wide variety of aspirations and abilities. College might include vocational training and experience, often in service to the institution itself, while teaching Latin and literature. The work of these women had feet in each camp, but might best reflect the sentiments of Du Bois at his most inclusive: "Education among all kinds of men always has had, and always will have, an element of danger and revolution, of dissatisfaction and discontent. Nevertheless, men strive to know."[2]

Not all reformers whose perspectives emphasized postsecondary education beyond normal or industrial schooling actually found themselves involved in higher education settings. Some, such as Palmer Memorial Institute founder Charlotte Hawkins Brown, worked primarily at the foundational level where they could prepare students for collegiate possibilities. Although Palmer announced a "course of instruction of a double nature" in academic and industrial subjects, its recruitment literature boasted about those students who had ultimately become college graduates in dentistry, theology, medicine, pharmacy, and education. Palmer proudly advertised itself as "the only college preparatory school of its type in America for Negro youth" and even added the tag line on informational materials, "a little bit of New England in North Carolina."[3]

Another African American female educator, Anna Julia Cooper, argued vociferously for an intellectually challenging curriculum, including classical subjects, as college preparation for black students at the Washington, D.C., M Street High School, where she served as principal from 1902 to 1906. One of the first black females to earn a Ph.D., Cooper clashed significantly with the District of Columbia Board of Education on the subject of academic college preparation for African Americans. She continued to remain uncompromising about meaningful higher education opportunities for blacks and women while serving in faculty and administrative capacities at Lincoln University, Jefferson City, MO, during the early twentieth century.[4]

Others seeking to reform southern education with an eye toward postsecondary learning worked directly to create or enhance institutions of higher education. In Birmingham, Julia Tutwiler was responsible for opening the University of Alabama to coeducation. Alice Lloyd founded a junior college in the remote reaches of Kentucky with a curriculum she categorized simply as "prelaw," "arts and sciences," and "normal" to fit her aim "to train leaders who will remain in the mountains and serve their people."[5]

The women whose vision for educational reform settled on postsecondary education are depicted in lives that share some similarities and many differences. Most striking in the first category are the early personal paths that sparked their interests in guiding change at the collegiate level. Perhaps illuminating much of what we know about the roots of reform and reformers, the stories of the women motivated to contribute in this arena are stories of sticking close to what worked in their own lives. These educational reformers appear to have selected their reform targets and/or methods with high regard for what they knew from experience or dreamed of experiencing.

Each of the female collegians discussed in this chapter had secondary education that was college preparatory in nature and at least some direct experience with education beyond the secondary level. They may have longed for more. For example, Charlotte

Hawkins Brown, after graduating from the Cambridge (MA.) English High School in 1900, set her sights on college at Radcliffe. Family financial realities forced a revision of that goal, but Brown did manage postsecondary education at the state normal school at Salem, MA. Just seven years older than Brown, Alice Lloyd attended Boston's Chauncy Hall, a coeducational elite college preparatory school, and also managed several years at Radcliffe.[6]

Julia Tutwiler, whose accomplishments in Alabama ranged from improvements in the statewide prison system to the presidency of Livingston Normal College and the inclusion of female students at the University of Alabama, clearly understood higher education. Her father was in the first class to enter the University of Virginia and taught at the University of Alabama before founding a boys college preparatory school. When her brother was a student at Washington and Lee College, she accompanied him to Lexington, Virginia, to receive private tutoring in Latin and Greek from college faculty. She attended Vassar College for a year and received a German teaching certificate after attending Deaconesses' Institute near Dusseldorf.[7]

Other college level contributors of the era included Elizabeth Avery Colton, a prominent force in raising the academic standards of women's colleges in the South and a graduate of Statesville (NC) Female College who also attended Mount Holyoke and received bachelor's and master's degrees, in 1903 and 1905, from Teachers College of Columbia University. Katherine Bowersox, the influential and indefatigable dean of women at Berea College for most of the first half of the twentieth century, received her postsecondary training at Bloomsburg (PA) Literary Institute and State Normal School.[8]

Clearly, these women and many others who influenced the course of higher education in the South early in the twentieth century understood the need for students to strive beyond literacy and basic skill training. Their aspirations for their students were lodged in terms like economic independence, social responsibility, intellectual maturity, aesthetic appreciation, and community leadership. Their experience convinced them that the achievement of these aspirations could best happen in postsecondary settings committed to academic rigor, high social standards, and discipline. Admirably, women who experienced at least some college or college preparatory work—often as first generation women of higher education in their families—sought leadership roles in education so that others could be trained to lead in their spheres of interest. These women were not inclined to climb the ladder and pull it up after them, but rather to use their summits to stop and build bigger and better ladders for those behind them.

The eye toward future community leaders was consistent with a philosophical perspective apparent among the women working in the southern higher education arena. They saw education as not just a benevolent exercise but a political force—an instrument for renegotiating the balance of power and influence. In this regard, and perhaps because of personal experience, these women viewed their work at the intersection of social and economic circumstances forged by gender, class, and race. Their aims were situated not only in the lives of those they directly touched, but also in a generational chain of uplift for communities and groups that most needed it. If work toward such objectives can be called "progressive," it is progressive more in terms of social reform than social service. Did the reform impulse imply control? Certainly, these were women who believed it was time for disenfranchised groups—the black, the female, the rural poor—to gain greater control of their own destinies.

However, it is likely that the women educational reformers of the South had little time or patience for the darker manipulations of planned control. Their work was highly opportunistic and focused on the immediacy of their endeavors. Pedagogical details were less important than philosophical underpinnings; and educational thought was less important than educational action. An interesting paradox appears when we consider how these women did or did not view education as an instrument for extending democracy. On one hand, they aimed their efforts at disenfranchised groups and individuals, creating opportunities for those who had not had them. These were the opportunities that could resonate in families and communities for generations. On the other hand, however, their actual teaching tended toward personal and local improvements. There is scant indication of schooling situated in the notion of a world community of democratic intent and multiple inclusion. More attention was aimed at "our people," "your opportunities," and "this community" than at widespread democratic ideals.

Typically, the southern women working to enhance higher education opportunities found themselves alternately calling upon skills of confrontation and skills of compromise. While they needed support from benefactors whose motives might be to keep the disenfranchised in their respective places, they also needed to motivate those disenfranchised to strive for other places. This dichotomy is particularly clear in the case of Charlotte Hawkins Brown, founder of the Alice Freeman Palmer Memorial Institute, an African American all grades school with teacher and industrial training, agricultural and home economics courses, college preparatory studies, and, eventually, a junior college. Brown's corporate charter for the school in Sedalia, NC, could be viewed as a study in the far reaches of accommodation, testifying that the aim of the corporation was to conduct "an institution for the education of the colored race...to teach said colored race improved methods of agriculture and industrial pursuits generally."[9]

Although such statements of intent netted Booker T. Washington as a friend of the school who lent his name to fund-raising efforts, they did not prevent Brown from quickly fashioning a curriculum along the lines of her own at Cambridge High School work, including literature, history, foreign languages, grammar, music, art, and geography. Later, she would characterize Palmer as "college preparatory based on New England standards."[10]

Charlotte Hawkins Brown and the Palmer Institute

Such contradictory postures—sometimes retreating, sometimes advancing—may have been easier for Charlotte Hawkins Brown to manage than most. Her own experiences had put her in contact with many more whites than would have been typical for a black citizen of Henderson, NC, born in 1883, and she well understood that the route from A to B was not a straight line for blacks operating in a white world. "Lottie" Hawkins was the granddaughter of a favored and fair-skinned plantation slave, Rebecca, commonly thought to be the half white daughter of wealthy North Carolina planter and lawyer John D. Hawkins. Lottie's mother, Carrie, born after emancipation as the twelfth child of Rebecca and her husband Mingo, was schooled in white social and cultural advantages while reared in the Raleigh home of Rebecca's white half sister, Jane A. Hawkins. Miss Jane had determined to turn the precocious Carrie into a cultured "colored lady." After a great deal of success in the area of culture, religion, and manners, as well as some academic schooling, the plan ended when 16-year-old Carrie became pregnant and moved to her mother's ample house in a well-kept middle-class section of Henderson.[11]

The atmosphere in the birth home of Charlotte Hawkins Brown created a backdrop for cultural and intellectual achievement. There were exterior columns. There was a piano. There was cleanliness and space. Still, even upwardly mobile blacks were far from equal to whites in opportunity. Jim Crow laws, fear of lynchings, limited job possibilities, inadequate educational provisions, and white contempt restricted their freedom and their futures. Joining the black migration North to seek opportunities unknown in the South, 19 members of the Hawkins family moved to Boston in 1888. They settled in Cambridge, renting homes in a townhouse neighborhood that was a melting pot of middle-class African Americans and ethnic groups representing all spectrums of recent European immigration. Charlotte's mother married fellow transplanted Carolinian Nelson Willis, sublet rooms to other African American arrivals from the South, including Harvard students, and opened a laundry in the basement. Willis worked as an unskilled laborer—generally as a janitor or handyman-and Charlotte attended Allston Grammar School, then Cambridge English High School.[12]

A combination of parental guidance, community influence, and personal inclination and ability during the formative Cambridge years shaped not only the individual that Charlotte Hawkins Brown would become, but also the factors she would emphasize in the development of her future students. She readily determined that great poise and high intellect were crucial keys to forward movement among the youth of her race. After all, they had worked for her. Here, it would be easy to suggest that Brown was "selling out" by adapting the social and cultural trappings of educated whites. She shed the nickname "Lottie" and became known as Charlotte Eugenia Hawkins. Favored with natural musical ability, she took voice and piano lessons. At church, she took advantage of opportunities to showcase her public speaking skills. Her manners and dress were no different from upper-class white adolescents and teenagers. However, what may appear as a careful attempt to fit in by imitation was more likely the natural product of an environment that found Brown in the company of a majority of fellow students who were white and, as she recalled in later years, never made her feel different. "No teacher or student ever made me uncomfortable in any way," she insisted. "I knew nothing of segregation; there were no barriers of which I was conscious."[13]

Carrie Hawkins Willis was determined that her daughter acquire good social graces and personal values, and much of this was accomplished through involvement in Cambridge's all black Union Baptist Church. Through her church involvement, an impressionable 14-year-old Brown was present to hear Booker T. Washington lecture on "The Negro in the South," in which he exhorted the fortunate blacks of Boston to return South to help their less fortunate brothers and sisters.[14]

The woman who would found an educational institution variously referred to as a college preparatory school and a finishing school was not disinclined toward the Washington emphasis on black economic uplift through vocational preparation. Later she would explain:

> Dr. Washington, as a man known by his intimates, hated segregation, unjust discrimination, though apparently he bore them with patience and tolerance. Why? Because he felt that the humanitarianism in his white neighbors would lift them above the petty things that had made them an object of ridicule so often to the rest of the nation. He admonished his South with these burning words: "No man can keep another man in the ditch without remaining there himself." But his greatest philosophy, which we shall do well to practice today in this life and death struggle, is one found in the immortal quotation of his, "No man shall drag me so low as to make me hate him."[15]

Brown and many others saw Washington more as a pacifist than an accommodationist. When she heard his plea for helping hands in the South, she heard only a stirring and passionate force for bettering the lives of the most needy of Americans—the African Americans in the South. When she heard his response to discrimination, she heard only the voice of an uplifted spirit on the high road to passive change. Brown, and many others, undoubtedly viewed gradual means as justifying the eventual ends. She found nothing incongruent with her own methods which would eventually draw on elements of both Washington and DuBois to develop a school that could garner support among white donors while meeting the broad intellectual needs of black youths who might become academic and community leaders.

Cambridge provided Brown with opportunities unknown to southern African Americans. The unique college town, a melting pot of ethnic variety and academic acumen, also exposed her to a number of important role models and northern white supporters. Maria L. Baldwin was serving as the African American principal of Boston's elite and primarily white Agassiz Grammar School. She had gained a reputation as an exceptional educator; and as an early role model for Brown, she "gave great courage to my desire to forge ahead and become."[16] Brown discovered another role model when she heard a talk in church about the work of Lucy Craft Laney, graduate in the first class of Atlanta University and founder of the Augusta, GA, Haines Normal and Industrial School, a multidimensional school that filled an enormous need for African American education in that corner of the Jim Crow

South. Speaking later of Laney, Brown maintained "her achievement in spite of her color determined my career as an educator and builder."[17]

While a senior in high school and babysitting for extra money, Brown met Alice Freeman Palmer, a founder of the American Association of University Women and president of Wellesley College. When Palmer passed Brown on a Cambridge street, the young babysitter was pushing a baby carriage with one hand while studying a copy of *Virgil* held in the other. She stopped to ask Brown about her school and soon after inquired about her identity to the school's principal. Later, when Brown's mother had discouraged her notions of a Radcliffe education in favor of two-year training in a normal school, Brown found Palmer's name listed as a member of the state board of education on literature about the state normal school at Salem. She wrote to Palmer, reminding her of their one chance meeting and mentioning her interest in normal schooling. Palmer's unexpected reply was an offer of financial assistance that enabled Brown to attend the normal school at Salem.

Charlotte Hawkins Brown was one of many capable normal school students who received work opportunities before they received their certificates of graduation. A conversation on a train with a representative of the American Missionary Association led Brown to a position as an AMA missionary teacher at Bethany Institute, a small rural church and school about ten miles east of Greensboro, NC. When Brown arrived in 1901, Bethany had just been granted normal school status by the AMA. Its teaching staff included Brown and Malsie D. Green. Reverend Manuel L. Baldwin served as minister and principal of the tiny all-grades school on a dirt path into pine forests.

Brown and her family had traveled regularly from Boston to North Carolina for Christmas visits with relatives still there, but the new teacher was hardly prepared for the depths of rural poverty and isolation she confronted at Bethany. Although she made some headway with curriculum changes geared to bringing students up to grade levels and with converting an old blacksmith shop into student housing to assure better attendance among students who lived many miles from school, a financially strapped AMA decided to close Bethany the following year. This event, along with the sudden death of Alice Freeman Palmer in 1902, sparked Brown's plans to raise funds for her own school, the Alice Freeman Palmer Memorial Institute (Palmer Institute) in Sedalia, NC.[18]

Brown's very general aim for her all-grades boarding school was racial uplift-the improvement of the lives of black citizens in any walk of life. She viewed education as the centrifugal force that could keep all elements essential to that uplift working together, including: social refinement, self discipline, moral and religious lifestyle, aesthetic appreciation, work preparation, and general subject education. From time to time, depending on circumstances and audiences, Brown emphasized one element over another, as when she insisted to her students, "Acquire manners, the rest will come."[19] The early curriculum at Palmer Institute would surface as a potpourri of offerings that reflected Brown's personal preferences and Latin school education, as well as rural economic needs and traditional southern values. Agriculture, home economics, music, literature, languages, and mathematics were among the training programs and academic subjects included in the curriculum, along with classes in morals and manners. The upper grades eventually included teacher training, an element which qualified the school for county funds. When the Smith-Hughes Act passed in 1917, federal funding helped to subsidize Palmer's industrial classes.[20]

All southern women who would seek reform in postsecondary or private education needed to be expert fund raisers—especially among northern benefactors. Brown was fortunate in her New England contacts and freely approached former schoolmates, friends of friends, and other educators. She also approached affluent northerners who frequented hunting lodges in the area. Frances Guthrie, an enthusiastic early supporter from New York, had distinct ideas for a Palmer curriculum based on her impressions of the limited abilities and futures of African American youth. Her suggestions to Brown demonstrated the kinds of predicaments that Brown and others faced when they dealt with some of their valued donors. Guthrie warned Brown that her students "are not like you, they have not had your upbringing" and it would be a mistake to try to teach them "more than their heads are ready to receive." Convinced that rural whites and blacks were "nearly all very ignorant people," Guthrie suggested practical training in life skills, such as cleanliness and manners, as well as Bible teachings. "Essential reading and writing skills could be achieved concurrently through topics such as 'How I Clean a Room'."[21]

While everything in Brown's experience suggested an uncompromising regard for learning at the highest levels, she undoubtedly understood that a great deal of preparatory work was essential to move rural students from hard scrabble farms to Howard or Harvard. This reality readily complemented the paternalistic impulses of white philanthropists whose checkbooks typically opened only to assist in teaching good behavior, religion, and industrial competencies to African Americans. It also fit well with Brown's own maternal instinct to teach healthy life styles, proper deportment, and even successful dress and speech.

Thus, Brown was willing to shape a multifaceted curriculum that spread into every type of learning and development likely to attract northern funds, satisfy the local community preferences, or speak to her own ideals. She was impatient to build buildings and recruit students, but she was patient in terms of curricular goals and careful to do what she felt the survival of the school dictated. By 1910, largely to the credit of its benevolent New England friends, Palmer Institute had extensive acreage, several wooden buildings, a new boys' dormitory, a school dairy farm, a domestic science cottage, just over 100 students, and five faculty members. Its students ranged from elementary to high school grades learning reading, writing, math, literature, grammar, history, and agriculture. For college or normal school preparatory students, there were advanced courses in education, government, and foreign languages. Among the seven students who graduated in 1909, two went on to become school principals, one a physician, one a pastor, and one a teacher.[22] One of the remaining two became a carpenter, the other a housekeeper. The school's motto reflected its multidimensional ends and means: "educational efficiency, spiritual sincerity, and cultural security."[23]

As Palmer Institute grew, so did the demands for funds. Brown was indefatigable in her appeals and her networking and quite willing to paint a picture of her school and her own philosophies that matched the preferences of any potential donor. For example, when she attended meetings of white club women to solicit support, she might emphasize the training of domestic labor at Palmer, where she noted that female students were preparing to be "fine clean mothers and good homemakers for themselves and others."[24]

Brown extended her work for African American uplift well beyond Palmer Institute, creating community service projects for her agriculture students and, in 1909, bringing the School Improvement League to Sedalia, with its community and school betterment efforts. Brown also built valuable networks with local churches, school agents, and business interests, as well as a fairly sophisticated fundraising campaign based on northern philanthropy. She sought to solidify local white support for the school by placing up to five such educators and businessmen on her Board of Directors. A tireless networker who understood that community and state support was needed to complement northern philanthropy, she was a founder of the North Carolina Federation of Negro Women's Clubs and served as its president from 1912 to 1922. Later, she served as president of the North Carolina Teachers Association.[25]

In 1911, Charlotte Hawkins married Edward Brown, who she had met a year earlier when he was a Harvard student who had rented a room at her mother's house in Cambridge. When Edward Brown moved to North Carolina to play second fiddle to his busy and highly focused wife, the marriage quickly began to falter. The couple separated in 1912 and divorced four years later, unable to reconcile her need to devote all her energies to her school and his desire to forge a career of his own. A second marriage, in 1923 to John Moses, a teacher at Palmer Institute, ended in annulment in less than a year.[26]

As Palmer moved into the second decade of its existence, Brown continued to seek out stable financial footing. Although she was unsuccessful in interesting the General Education Board in contributions and unable to convince the Guilford County School Board to make Palmer a county high school, she managed to raise thousands of dollars from northern benefactors who responded to her persistent letter writing campaigns and her articulate and persuasive personal pleas.

The curricular direction of Palmer Institute began to change in 1913, as both the school and its founder started a slow movement away from accommodationist practices and pretenses. The change was first marked by the interest of a new benefactor, New York financier Galen L. Stone. Not only did Stone donate substantial sums over the years, including funding for a large brick administration building, but he was the first northern white donor to encourage Brown to prepare her students to become leaders and citizens, not just African Americans with industrial jobs. Brown could talk to him candidly about her hopes and plans for her students, understanding that his interest in the school was more aligned with the philosophies of W.E.B. DuBois than with those of Booker T. Washington.[27]

By 1924, Palmer's recruitment literature boasted of its alumni who went on to college and professional schools. The school had grown to 214 students, mostly boarders, with property valued at $200,000 on over 300 acres. Palmer prided itself on being both "an accredited high school offering special instruction in fine and practical arts," and "the only college preparatory school of its type in America for Negro youth," as well as "a distinctive school of Christian culture."[28] Later, Brown added a junior college to the Palmer campus and emphasized both "finishing school" aims and transfer to four-year degree granting institutions.[29]

A paradox emerged in Brown's life and work around the issue of personal style and professional goals. Not surprisingly, the creation of an African American all-grades school and junior college for African Americans in an area of extreme rural poverty required a great deal of tenacity, cleverness, and personal fortitude. Brown fit the role as a smart and strong willed individual with energy and desire both to contribute and to control. She controlled every aspect of students' lives by dictating their dress, their deportment, their social and religious habits, and their academic lives. She controlled the development of the school by keeping a tight rein on finances, sharing selectively with the board of trustees, and personally managing all administrative and personnel issues.

The same stubborn tenacity that enabled Brown to build Palmer Institute into a place of opportunity for those who otherwise had none, could readily alienate the school's supporters. For example, when Brown approached Guilford County about putting the school on a stable foundation by making it a county public school, she insisted that she would need to continue to control all its affairs. Quite naturally, the Board of Education did not see this as a workable arrangement. Brown did reach an agreement for the American Missionary Association to take over the school in 1927, while leaving her in substantial operational control. However, six years later, continuing problems in the relationship ended in its termination.[30]

Brown's uncompromising nature surfaced again when she refused the advice of her northern benefactors about her fund raising campaigns and the nature of her expenditures. As some board members began questioning her abilities and their own involvement, one major benefactor sent his own accountant to the school and pleaded with Brown to stop spending money before she raised it.[31] Board member Edith MacFadden served as controller for several years in the early 1920's before she became frustrated with Brown's tight reins on financial administration. She characterized Brown to others as incompetent to run the school.[32]

In her role as a sought-after speaker and recognizable personality, Brown eventually trampled on the possibility that she was willing to compromise on a lesser role for educated African

American citizens. In an exemplary public speech to a primarily white audience at Berea College, she enumerated several of her visions:

> An opportunity for Negro youth in any and all vocations for which they show an aptitude; equal educational opportunities; a proper evaluation of human personality under black skin; the abolition of purely Negro jobs and an open door to earn a living with equal wages for equal work; the same respect for members of the Negro race that white people feel entitled to from the Negro race.[33]

Brown advanced in racial activism as her school advanced in prominence, and she became unwilling to turn the other cheek on insult. Of experiences on trains, she later recalled, "For years I was regularly put out of Pullman berths and seats during all hours of the night. Stranger than fiction is the fact that each time my southern lawyer, taking no percent of the recovery, sued and won. The sums were not large, for inconveniencing a Negro woman or humiliating her, in the eyes of the court, was never considered as any great outrage...." Brown became a vice president of the National Association of Colored Women and a member of numerous boards and commissions. In 1932, she received an honorary doctorate from Wilberforce Academy.[34]

By 1941, Palmer Institute advertised itself as "A Strictly College Preparatory School for Teen Age Boys and Girls," as well as "The School of Personal Charm: Where Manners Are a Part of the Daily Curriculum."[35] For Brown, the potential for acquiring social graces was as important as the academic training. Her continuing insistence to her students and others that there was one right way to speak, respond, sit, stand, walk, dress, and eat culminated in her self-published book, *The Correct Thing to Do, To Say, To Wear,* first released in 1940 and later commercially published by Christopher House, Boston, in 1941.[36]

Brown's book, a combination of etiquette instruction and parental nagging, initially was widely accepted by parents and teachers. Later, it was criticized as overly didactic and paternalistic, although accurately depicting "what Brown believed constituted the all-important edge for blacks in improving their relationships with whites and in convincing them of their right to equality."[37] Chapters included "Earmarks of a Lady," "Earmarks of a Gentleman," "How to Behave," "Poise," and "Helpful Hints for Correctness." Each was largely comprised of lists of what to do and what not to do. For example, a section on train travel included this list of admonishments:

1. Avoid carrying a great many bags with you.
2. Do not carry paper packages unless absolutely necessary.
3. Never carry a package wrapped in newspaper.
4. Avoid loud talking and boisterous laughing.
5. Do not chew gum. It is always bad taste to chew gum in public.
6. Do not use the train or public conveyance for grooming which should be done in private quarters.[38]

The Palmer campus was awash in rules that reflected Brown's push for correctness. The dress code required jackets for men, skirts for women. The students were restricted to limited intermingling across the sexes and were even divided by gender during programs in the auditorium. Strict rules were enforced about card playing, use of radios, visits home, trips into town, chapel attendance, and numerous other student activities. Brown became a noted purveyor of social graces whose lectures, radio speeches, and writing reached a wide national audience. Eventually, she wrote a weekly column, "The Correct Thing," for the *Norfolk (VA) Journal and Guide*.[39]

At Palmer Institute, the ideal of correctness became a niche in an educational market where historically black institutions like Howard and Morehouse were achieving academic accolades and where land grant colleges like South Carolina State and Virginia State were carving out technical and vocational territory. Even when lodged in the finishing school category, however, Palmer managed to retain substantial academic respectability and to develop into an institution described by one analyst as "certainly not what white supporters had in mind as 'practical' education for blacks. Instead, the school imitated what whites considered the best for their own children, offering a wide range of academic courses plus extra-curricular activities which included European study trips and participation in the acclaimed Sedalia Singers."[40]

Speaking to a strictly black audience in *The Brown America*, Joseph Baker pointed out, "Palmer is a finishing school—and while that phrase has been used with varying degrees of respect as far as Negroes are concerned, it has taken on a new and solid meaning....To Charlotte Hawkins Brown, 'finishing' means just what it says; and she is knocking off the warpings and straightening out the kinks found too often in post-mature years in Negro leadership."[41] In *Ebony* Palmer was applauded for its "high scholastic standard equivalent to a first class New England prep school." [42]

By 1952, when Brown turned over the reins of Palmer to her successor, Wilhelmina Crosson, the school was highly selective, deliberately small (200 students), home to a student body drawn from 24 states, and able to claim a campus valued at nearly one million dollars. Speaking at Crosson's inauguration as the second president of Palmer Institute, Brown asked that she continue a school "where good breeding and good English play a major part. I want pupils to be courteous; and to be good students...."[43]

Brown died in 1961 and her school, buckling under the weight of financial burdens and increased competition for students, closed in 1971. However, the place of the Alice Freeman Palmer Memorial Institute as an enduring model of educational uplift initiated by a single, determined woman remains secure.

Alice Lloyd, Martha Berry, and Colleges for Appalachia

While Charlotte Hawkins Brown worked to create opportunities for African Americans in rural North Carolina, other women were moved by social betterment ideals to test the possibilities of educational improvement in Appalachia. Motivated by widespread stories of impoverished and isolated families living in windowless cabins off hard scrabble farming, these women generally arrived from New England or from other parts of the South. Unlike

Brown, the women who focused their work on the mountainous regions of the southern states could not legitimately claim their targeted population as "their people." Intrigued, even romanced, by Appalachian cultural distinctions, many of them viewed education as much a vehicle for preserving and maximizing local ways as a force for individual improvement and widespread democratic uplift.

In broad terms, however, similarities did occur among women working to extend educational access at every level to various isolated southern populations—whether in the coal girdled hills of eastern Kentucky or the lowland marshes of coastal South Carolina. Most prominently, the women working in Appalachia shared with Brown and other southern educational reformers middle- and upper-class white value systems; earnest beliefs in the necessity of an educated citizenry; desires to enhance the social welfare of those less fortunate; and personal philosophical orientations variously marked by both traditionalism and reform. Within these similarities there remained ample room for divergent means, and even ends, related to their educational endeavors, as well as some individual philosophical inconsistencies that allowed each to shape very different experiences and institutions.

Like Brown at Sedalia, the women who created new programs and institutions among southern highlanders quickly realized that any missionary and denominational support for their initial endeavors needed more stable undergirding over time. However, support from large philanthropic foundations and the General Education Board largely was reserved for efforts aimed at broad-based improvements, rather than isolated local projects. Along with their counterparts working throughout the South, women attempting to build educational institutions in Appalachia relied on force of personality to approach wealthy individuals one at a time for support for their causes. Personal communication of a compelling message was the most essential weapon in the struggle to garner resources for funding their schools. Martha Berry, for example, successfully befriended the Carnegie and Ford families on behalf of the Berry Colleges which she founded near Rome,

GA. Alice Lloyd, for her Caney Junior College (later renamed Alice Lloyd College) in eastern Kentucky, received regular financial support from two spinster sisters in Passaic, NJ, and tapped her fellow classmates from Boston's Chauncy Hall School and Radcliffe College. Both also raised thousands of dollars through well-targeted mail campaigns and even cold calls throughout the communities surrounding their schools.[44]

Alice Geddes Lloyd, born in Athol, MA, in 1876, and Martha McChesney Berry, born 10 years earlier in Rome, GA, could be viewed as somewhat typical of women of means, intelligence, and independence whose interests were sparked by the social ideals so vividly demonstrated in Jane Addams' urban settlement work. In the case of Berry, those interests were further solidified by first-hand knowledge of conditions among the hill country citizens not far from her own home.

The work of Lloyd and Berry represents one of three major areas of endeavor, often intertwined, undertaken by women who pursued economic and social enhancement among the mountain people. The first of these, community settlements, were catch-all centers for endeavors to support local uplift, ranging from handicraft making to socializing and from adult education to Sunday school. One significant thrust of the settlements that dotted the hills and hollows was cultural preservation-the promotion of heritage traditions in mountain handicrafts, ballads, oral histories, musical instruments, dances, and the like. Much of the preservation work was pursued through settlement centers or schools that also sought to promote social interaction and teach contemporary life skills.[45]

For example, May Stone and Katherine Pettit, founders of the Hindman Settlement School in eastern Kentucky, promoted both training in typically middle-class menu preparation and nutrition as well as traditional rafia weaving. Appalachian scholar David E. Whisnant concluded, "Paradoxically, for all their professed reverence for traditional culture and their wish to forestall the cultural effects of impending industrialization, the settlement school women were themselves powerful instigators of cultural change."

When Katherine Pettit teamed with Ethel De Long Zande to found the Pine Moutain Settlement School in 1913, conservation of tradition mixed with vocational training, home economics, and some determined progressive pedagogy to prepare mountain people for a life that both honored their cultural distinctiveness and prepared them for contemporary marketplace realities.[46]

A second area of effort brought to the region focused on establishing handicraft industries, collectives that organized and sold the local wares that could be produced in profitable quantity as regionally representative. Endeavors to organize indigenous craft output for profit often were undertaken by women whose particular interests largely were aimed at economic advancement for the region. Frances Louisa Goodrich, for example, came to Buncombe County, NC, in 1890 as a mission worker for the Woman's Board of Home Missions of the Presbyterian Church. There she found some distinctive hand-loomed coverlets, developed specifications for standardizing the most pleasing of the patterns, and organized local residents into groups of spinners, weavers, and dyers whose wares were soon regularly shipped North. Next, with yarns and designs selected for market demand, Goodrich organized the Cottage Industries Guild of Allanstand, NC. Eventually she moved its operations, including centralized workshops and a showroom, to Asheville, NC. This type of entrepreneurial agency on behalf of local craft makers inevitably spread to the production of rugs, brooms, willow baskets, woolen blankets, and palmetto hats.[47]

The work that engaged Lloyd and Berry was oriented toward a third focus of the Appalachian uplift activities pursued by socially conscious outsiders: traditional schooling for those who had little or none within reach. Although training to enhance local practices in fields such as agriculture and home economics was readily accepted as part of that education, it was not necessarily central. Religious piety, personal hygiene, morality, citizenship, and basic academic subjects were far more prominent as these women built their one-room schools into fully accredited colleges. For Berry, who started her program as a Sunday school for nearby children, the shift to academic and vocational fare came naturally as numbers increased and lack of adequate schooling became apparent. For Lloyd, whose work in Kentucky began with development of community civic and social betterment activities, the move to concentrate on the development of an educational institution occurred when "it became apparent, at least to Lloyd, that the region's educational needs were more pressing. The local primary school was inadequate; there was no high school within reasonable reach; and a college education was deemed irrelevant for all but a tiny handful."[48]

Alice Geddes Lloyd, born Alice Spencer Geddes, came to her work in Kentucky more from a commitment to benevolent deeds than a commitment to educational reform. In this respect, her path initially was similar to many educated club women of her native Massachusetts, where the spirit of female heroism in settlement work so readily complemented the "new woman" image of independence and self support. Lloyd, who lived with her grandmother in Cambridge, MA, during her teenage years, while her father's work transferred him to England, was raised in upper middle-class surroundings and schooled at Chauncy Hall and Cambridge Latin college preparatory schools. Although she spent approximately two years at Radcliffe College, she did not earn a degree. She learned independence and persistence during those formative years when she traveled frequently to Europe to visit her parents, participated actively in women's clubs in the Boston area, and suffered a bout with polio that left her partially paralyzed on the right side.[49]

Lloyd was more fortunate than many independent and educated women of her time who generally found the pool of relevant employment opportunities to be pitifully shallow for women. Many became teachers; a few worked as nurses; a growing number gravitated to social work. At age 22, Lloyd (still Alice Geddes) was delighted to land a job as a cub reporter on the weekly *Cambridge Chronicle*, and within a year she had initiated a regular section on women's interests. Five years later, she joined with two women friends to buy their own weekly, *The Cambridge Press*, an entrepreneurial venture that lasted only 15 months. Lloyd then became assistant editor of another local weekly paper and later launched her career as an active freelance writer, a teacher of writing courses, and a lecturer on various issues and causes. She continued to live with her grandmother in upper middle-class Boston and its suburbs until the elderly Mrs. Geddes died in 1909.[50]

When Alice Spencer Geddes joined her widowed mother, Ella Geddes, on a summer vacation in New Hampshire, they were guests of Arthur Lloyd. In 1914, she married Lloyd, moved to New Hampshire, brought her mother with her, and hit her stride in benevolent community outreach work among the rural poor. Lloyd's activities, by all accounts also enthusiastically embraced by Arthur Lloyd, included initiation of a community lending library, organization of a Child Welfare League, collection and distribution of used clothes to the poor, and development of a women's craft market. In seemingly equal measure, her efforts were welcomed by some and considered paternalistic and meddlesome by others. Community objections were strong enough to motivate the Lloyds to look for other areas of the country in need of good works. They would eventually settle on the remote hills of western Kentucky as an outlet for their energies and ideas, an area that Alice Lloyd described as "shut in on all sides" and marked by people who lived in "decadence and deterioration."[51]

A variety of romantic myths have surfaced about Alice Lloyd's arrival in Kentucky, some of them undoubtedly fueled by Lloyd herself. An article about Lloyd in a 1940 issue of *Time* magazine reported that she fled to Kentucky with $10 in cash to recover from a nervous breakdown. The *Reader's Digest* version in 1954 portrayed her as a sickly woman who had "driven from Boston in a buggy, the last remnant of the family's fortune. All else that she owned was in a trunk strapped on the back." A nostalgic memoir by former student Robert W. Sloane tells of a three-week trip by Alice Lloyd and her mother, all by horse-drawn buggy, following a doctor's orders that Lloyd should seek a milder climate and isolation for her fragile health. Alice Lloyd's chief assistant at the college, June Buchanan, noted that Lloyd was chronically ill from birth and decided to head for Kentucky after four doctors told her she had very little time left to live.[52]

These accounts ignored the active and energetic—far from frail—Alice Lloyd observed by her Boston and New Hampshire acquaintances. Nor did they note how a family with a comfortable life style and real estate holdings suddenly became penniless. Perhaps even more interesting, none of these popular versions mentioned Arthur Lloyd, who indeed accompanied his wife and mother-in-law to Kentucky, where they had been told of an abandoned Presbyterian mission in Knott County and offered an available cabin. In fact, Arthur Lloyd was as active as his wife in founding a community center in the town of Ivis, KY, where they first lighted. He was also involved in initiating similar activities a year later, 12 miles away in more remote Caney Creek, where he and local residents built a cabin for himself and the two Lloyd women.

Robert Sloane, a native of the Caney Creek region of Knott County who was seven years old when the Lloyds arrived, described the rugged isolation of the area in the early twentieth century as,

> one of Appalachia's most isolated regions, which for centuries had been ravaged by the twin evils of poverty and illiteracy. Feature, if you will, great stretches of mountains and valleys with no highways nor telephones, nor any of the comforts of modern living which we now think of as being absolute necessities. In this section, as is generally true throughout all Appalachia, educational levels were low, public schools were few, poorly equipped, and lasted only a few months during the seasons when the children were not needed for hoeing and digging and planting....The place, headwaters of Caney Creek, emptied some fifteen miles to the north into a branch of the Big Sandy River. Remote it was at the time of Mrs. Lloyd's arrival. The roads, as such, were dried rocky creek beds with two or three hours travel time to the nearest doctor. It was a full day's trip to the nearest grocery store in the county seat unless one used entirely the little country stores stocked with meal, flour, salt, coffee, and a scattered assortment of canned goods.[53]

The Caney Creek Civic Betterment Association, founded by the Lloyds in 1917, quickly established a used clothing and crop cooperative exchange, a library, a community service club, a farm improvement program, a federal post office, and a drive to build and staff one-room schools in neighboring communities. Alice Lloyd even gave the area an official town name: Pippa Passes, after the title of a Robert Browning poem. Many mountain neighbors, accustomed to close-knit relationships untouched by strangers, were suspicious of the Lloyds' eager good will. However, schooled in the difficulties of establishing relationships with rural New Hampshire communities, Alice and Arthur Lloyd now better understood how to slowly garner support, establish a broad base of participation, and strategically involve influential community members.[54]

Nevertheless, Lloyd's style could be highly directive and controlling. She was convinced that she knew best what the mountain people needed, including better hygiene and better breeding to create future generations untainted by intermarriage. To encourage improved housing, for example, she undertook the development of a homesteading project for a number of new two- and three-room cabins near the Community Center, which initially existed as a small plot of land donated by local resident Abisha Johnson. Future owners of the homes Lloyd dubbed "dream houses" built the residences with their own labor and with timber and other materials provided by the Caney Creek Civic Betterment Association. They then made small monthly house payments, accepted in cash, produce, or labor. Owners' contracts required them to allow regular home inspections, participate in the Caney Creek Community Club, work at some useful labor for the Community Center, treat livestock humanely, and give up drinking and shooting.[55] Alice Lloyd had a knack for exacting promises in exchange for goods and services.

After nearly three years, Arthur Lloyd left his wife and mother-in-law to continue on community work at Caney Creek on their own. According to Alice Lloyd, the break up of their marriage was occasioned by her discovery that her husband had for some time been in love with her best friend. Mrs. Geddes decided to stay on and became the postmistress of the Pippa Passes

Post Office. Alice Lloyd energized her community building efforts with extensive publicity and direct mail campaigns soliciting donations and volunteers. She also moved education to the top of her agenda and acquired an invaluable assistant, June Buchanan, who arrived in 1919 after graduating from Syracuse University and undertaking graduate work at Wellesley College.[56]

In addition to providing badly needed help with educational ideas and practices, June Buchanan was able to provide some essential financial backing. If the Community Center was to grow beyond the original small buildings on the land donated by Abisha Johnson and if it were to include enhanced educational opportunities, resources were needed to expand. Buchanan's father, initially skeptical but eventually taken by his daughter's enthusiasm, provided a gift of $1,500, which allowed her to buy the adjoining farm. Soon, a six-room schoolhouse was under construction to provide more grades and a more varied curriculum than were available in the one-room schoolhouses that offered the only accessible educational opportunities. The high school (jointly run by the Caney Creek Community Center and Knott County) soon became one of only two fully accredited class A high schools in the county.[57]

Lloyd moved quickly to expand into the college business, possibly motivated by the idea that any very bright students who graduated from the high school and went away to college would have limited commitment to their community roots. If they went to college right in Pippa Passes, they were more likely to become the future leaders in the general area. Local leadership, Lloyd decided, was the key to Appalachian uplift. While she had discovered generous and supportive citizens in the local community, she had found few local residents who were capable of dealing effectively with government bureaucracies, legal requirements, or business interactions on any large scale. Undoubtedly referring to the vast regional changes occurring with the growing coal industry, Lloyd wrote in one of the college handbooks, "If the mountaineer expects to control his own natural resources, he must equip himself immediately with a workable knowledge of business finance."[58] If the capacity to assure enduring, systemic improvements was not to be found among those already in residence, Lloyd would build it from among the local youngsters.

As her biographer David Searles pointed out, Alice Lloyd faced a daunting task in starting a college under any circumstances. But the burden was even more extreme when Caney Junior College opened in 1923 because, "The women heading the effort had not relevant experience, no buildings to house a college, and, as always, no money to pay the added costs." Nevertheless, the college began with a freshman class of two and a dean, V. Mignon Couser. In its first several years, it represented little more than extra work beyond high school courses, with individual tutoring toward continuation at other colleges.[59]

The high school had managed on local contributions and funds from Lloyd's friends and contacts in New England. Additionally, Lloyd had tapped into the benevolent sentiments of smart, upper-class young women who graduated from various New England colleges heady with ideas of social reform. Many responded to the publicity Lloyd was able to generate and signed on as volunteer teachers for a year or two. With a college and increased needs for physical facilities on the drawing boards, Lloyd redoubled her fund-raising campaign, largely dipping into her own well of friends from Radcliffe and various Boston women's clubs, then approaching her newspaper and magazine contacts for publicity. Unlike college founders Charlotte Hawkins Brown and Martha Berry, however, she emphasized direct mail to the masses over direct contact with targeted wealthy donors. Even with predictable setbacks during the depression, she managed to eventually develop a six million dollar endowment for Caney Creek Junior College. When Lloyd visited clubs and churches outside the region, she regularly took a group of students with her to present skits and tell stories about mountain life in a traveling show Lloyd labeled "The Forgotten Child Crusade."[60]

Not surprisingly, Lloyd arranged the selection and responsibilities of the trustees of the school in ways that maximized her own control. And she exacted an unwritten pledge from all students that in return for a free education they would stay in the Appalachian region or return to it to serve as capable leaders and exemplary citizens. Eventually, if she needed exemplars, she could turn to Caney Junior College graduate Carl D. Perkins, who returned after leaving for additional education, represented eastern Kentucky in the U.S. Congress for many years, and crafted legislation that would help hundreds of thousands more students fund their college educations.[61]

Caney Junior College was developed with a transition, not terminal, goal. Students would qualify themselves for acceptance into four-year colleges where they would seek education in professions that shaped the nature of their future contribution to the area. Lloyd particularly favored law, medicine, and education as end goals for her students. In keeping with the actions of other women who founded small colleges at the time, Lloyd turned to her own postsecondary educational experiences to fashion the two-year curriculum. In her case, it emphasized a rigorous liberal arts curriculum that could provide a foundation for multiple future directions.

"School should not be a vacation," insisted Lloyd, maintaining her college had "no place for manual training, typing, home economics, where the hands work harder than the head."[62] Instead, the Caney Creek Junior College course offerings included Latin (five courses), French, Spanish, biology, chemistry, physics, education, art, music, philosophy, economics, history, sociology, and literature, among others. In addition to the 64 credit hours necessary for graduation, students were required to work for the school. At the outset, students were responsible for most of the labor that built a number of the school's large wooden plank buildings. Faculty turnover was an ongoing problem, and even a few years of the difficult mountain life required great dedication. Nevertheless, among the sixteen men and women listed as faculty members in 1928, several were graduates of Columbia University Teacher's College; and others held graduate degrees from University of Michigan, Ohio University, Colorado State University, and Iowa State University.[63]

Applicants were interviewed and selected by Alice Lloyd who unabashedly sought qualities that fit her own image of leadership, although not necessarily the reality of an accomplished mountain native. Perhaps to Lloyd's credit, she did not emphasize standardized gauges of readiness for higher education, such as high school graduation. The high school at Caney Creek allowed the brightest children to push ahead as quickly as they could. They could then be examined by Lloyd and admitted to the junior college. In the case of Blanche Webb, admission occurred at age eleven.[64]

Perhaps the factor that most distinguished Lloyd from many social and educational reformers of her time was her wish to specifically reshape the population with which she involved herself. Like her counterparts in settlement houses, community centers, and schools, she wanted to maximize the potential of individuals and communities. But, unlike others, she believed that one route toward accomplishing that goal entailed encouraging basic changes in cultural aspects of the group she chose to serve. Most dramatically, Lloyd determined that some Appalachian bloodlines-particularly those marked by instances of intermarriage-seemed beyond improvement. The challenge was to use education for the uplift of individuals of good potential while working to strengthen the human stock for future generations. In this effort, Lloyd found support among followers of the eugenics movement that emphasized improved hereditary characteristics through attention to the genetic results of breeding practices.

Intermarriage, early marriage, and poor physical fitness, as well as lack of general education, were key targets in Lloyd's struggle for Appalachian improvement. "By reason of intermarriage and poor nourishment, many mountain boys and girls are not physically fit,"[65] she insisted. Lloyd did her part to curb the ills she saw by teaching health and hygiene, by establishing college selection processes that emphasized the most physically fit of the mountain stock, and by installing rules that prohibited informal contact between the sexes during the college years. In class, girls and boys sat in uniform on opposite sides of the room. Girls were forbidden to wear make-up or jewelry, and dates or casual conversations across the sexes were banned.[66]

Like Charlotte Hawkins Brown at Palmer Institute, Lloyd built a college environment steeped in formality, etiquette, discipline, and rules. Coincidentally, Lloyd also built a college embedded in the developmental philosophy of famed Harvard philosopher George Herbert Palmer, who she had met and admired and who was a valued friend of the college in North Carolina named in honor of his wife. Palmer's ideas, supported by a wellspring of puritanism, equated service to society as self interest, since the self exists in society. The preferred road to human completion started with self-knowledge and moved to self-sacrifice. In similar fashion, Caney Community College asked students to develop a worthy self, maximize intellectual capacity, and eventually return to the mountains to help lead others along the same path. George Herbert Palmer sent a note to Lloyd assuring her that the college was on firm philosophical footing.[67]

Although Caney Junior College managed to take root and slowly grow in the unlikely soil of one of Appalachia's poorest and most remote areas, Lloyd and her practices were not universally admired. At other mountain institutions, such as Berea College and Hindman settlement, she was seen as pushy and controlling with limited experience in either the academic world or the Appalachian culture. Ethel de Long Zande of Pine Mountain Settlement saw exploitation of children and perpetuation of mountaineer stereotypes in Lloyd's fund-raising tours. The American Missionary Association worried publicly about educational standards and careless administration. Berea College president William Hutchins disapproved of the educational methods employed.[68] Such criticisms undoubtedly were only partially grounded in real concerns. Some likely stemmed from Lloyd's own style, more stubborn than savvy, and from institutional rivalries over the scarce resources available to support benevolence in Appalachia.

Regardless of local objections and occasional ill will, Caney Creek College continued its existence, although marked by nearly constant financial crises. After Alice Lloyd's death in 1962, the college was renamed Alice Lloyd College. In 1980, it became an accredited four-year college, as it continues today. It has had an enormous impact on thousands of students who would not otherwise have had an opportunity for higher education; and the vast majority of those students graduated and went on to obtain degrees at four-year colleges, many beyond. As Alice Lloyd hoped, most graduates returned to the mountains to contribute to the area in a wide variety of ways.[69]

Several common threads among the women who exercised their progressive reform spirit in the initiation of new collegiate institutions can be viewed through the work of Martha Berry, founder of Berry College in Rome, GA. Like Brown and Lloyd, Berry was tenacious, single minded, and controlling. She shared their belief in extending education to the economically disadvantaged, not only to teach skills and hone the intellect, but also to teach a moral, disciplined way of life. Berry College, like Palmer Institute and Caney College, was a working demonstration model in appropriate behavior, service, on-site work participation, and community building. These institutions ignored many of the convictions held dear in the "progressive schools" being initiated as laboratories for the newest thinking in education, especially those concerning any emphasis on individual student interests. However, they inadvertently included a number of elements related to classroom community and social responsibility that might have made followers of John Dewey take note.

Martha Berry, whose personal style was schooled more in southern charm than New England rationalism, was more adept at softening doctrinaire tendencies than many determined female reformers of the era. Born just after the end of the Civil War, she grew up on the family plantation in Georgia's southern fringe of the Appalachian region. At home, she and her sisters learned from tutors and governesses. Later, her parents sent her to the Edgeworth Finishing School in Baltimore. Smart, energetic, and eager for some life focus, Berry came home to nurse her dying father and soon inherited a large estate. For reasons unknown, marriage, a high interest of her four sisters at the time, was not to happen for Martha Berry. Instead, she began informal Sunday school lessons for mountain children in the area of the family hunting lodge on Mt. Berry, GA, and from there built a boys' school, then a girls' school, and then a college.[70]

The Berry Schools started in 1902 in a cabin on Berry property that attracted a few lonely boys from the surrounding hills as boarding students who were taught by Martha Berry during the day, fed by her at meals, and told stories by her at bedtime. Tuition was paid in manual labor, and the initial emphasis was vocational and agricultural. Stanford graduate Elizabeth Brewster, and Berry's sister, Frances, signed on as teachers. Berry, like other women initiating new educational endeavors, was a natural builder. Within two years, 70 students, ages 12--23, were being served. Farming, carpentry, and forestry were among the first subjects taught and practiced; but quickly added to these were reading, math, chemistry, geography, debate, bible study, and music. The objective, according to Berry, was "to meet the educational and industrial needs of the poor white country boys of Georgia..., to make them independent, thrifty, and self-respecting."[71]

Berry acquired more land, built (with a great deal of student labor) more buildings, and added a girls' school in 1909. The Martha Berry School for Girls began with an emphasis on domestic skills, but Berry immediately began plans to add college preparatory programs for both the girls and boys. The full flowering of Berry's educational plans, eventually lodged on a campus expanded to 28,000 acres of scenic beauty, occurred in 1926 with the opening of a junior college. By 1930, Berry College was a full four-year postsecondary institution.[72]

Martha Berry provided one of the best examples of the personal characteristics that assisted Progressive Era women who sought to build educational institutions from the ground up. Although she was more fortunate than many others in having her own seed money and a locally prominent family, she quickly needed to exercise talents in persuasion, publicity, and tenacity to keep her endeavor afloat. In these areas, Berry was masterful. Undoubtedly, she learned early the value of well-placed friends; and she convinced a number of the area's most notable and well-connected businessmen to join her founding board of trustees. Their contacts netted her a visit from the governor of Georgia by the end of the boys' school's first year in operation, as well as introductions to potential wealthy donors. Not surprisingly, Berry soon found herself taking her appeals for funding to Philadelphia and New York. Her approach was well-practiced, persuasive, and eloquent, yet with a touch of southern sweetness (just short of vulnerability) that could captivate as well as convince.[73]

After briefly meeting Andrew Carnegie in 1907 at a dinner at the georgia Governor's mansion, Berry arranged to be on a train carrying Carnegie back to New York and to talk to him long enough to secure an invitation for a follow-up meeting in New York. That meeting led to a $50,000 donation to the boys' school and an introduction to Mrs. Russell Sage, who soon also became a donor. Berry, perhaps more than other women seeking northern philanthropy for southern reform efforts, made friends of her donors. Such was the case early on with Mr. and Mrs. Thomas Edison and eventually with Mr. and Mrs. Henry Ford. Beginning in the 1920s, the Fords visited Mt. Berry a number of times on their way to Florida, relaxing and even joining in student and faculty activities. Their contributions, eventually totaling nearly $4 million, were responsible for impressive Gothic-style buildings that dwarfed the original log and frame campus structures. Among other notable visitors who added materially to good publicity for the school were President Theodore Roosevelt (by then no longer in office), William McAdoo, and Gifford Pinchot.[74]

Typical of her fellow benevolent educators, Berry insisted that her schools include a great deal of strict discipline, correctness of demeanor, spiritual and physical cleanliness, and rigor in class work and campus service. Also typical, she was not universally beloved. Some locals objected to an institution so eager to rely on Yankee money. Others were suspicious of the students' manual labor commitment to the campus, charging that Berry had discovered how to get wealthy on free labor. Nevertheless, by the time she died in 1942, Berry was an educator who made a difference in thousands of lives and who received many national honors and awards. Back home in Georgia, she was appointed the first woman member of the State Board of University Regents.

Parallels and Paradoxes

The lives and works of women who contributed in the sphere of postsecondary liberal education during the Progressive Era can be investigated productively in terms of several questions. What do their lives say about the kind of women who undertook these endeavors? What does their work say about the elements necessary to assure the survival and continuance of these precarious institutions? What in their experiences leads them to certain curricular and pedagogical choices?

In search for an answer to each question, the key may very well be the necessity of compromise and the response to that necessity. For Progressive Era women, disenfranchised from meaningful participation in political and economic life, socially conscious work was often the compromise that enabled useful contributions and outlets for educated minds. Many of these women had the makings of successful bankers, politicians, doctors, lawyers, or school superintendents. But these avenues were closed in a system that required them to compromise potential with possibility—a lucky compromise indeed for the women depicted in this chapter.

Perhaps the most obvious compromise was evident in the lack of successful marriages and families. Women who chose to build new institutions were women who would need to be single minded and fully engaged in their work. Marriages attempted easily fell apart. Families would have demanded as much time as schools. Charlotte Hawkins Brown came closest to managing a family life by taking in several nieces and nephews who lived with her as their substitute mother, including one niece who became the wife of musician Nat King Cole.

As noted earlier, these women educators needed to be tenacious, truly driven in their determination to create new educational options in the Progressive Era. One very compelling reason the rural poor and the African Americans had been virtually left out of the southern pattern of education was simply that people with money and influence didn't much care to see them educated. The women who tackled reform needs by founding institutions for these populations had to hold on long enough to locate people who did care or to convince those who didn't care that they should. To do that, they undoubtedly had to make many compromises in order to attract everything from local good will to county and state support. Then, as now, people who needed donors had to curb their inclinations and opinions to keep them happy. Martha Berry even found herself agreeing to a week of music and dancing at Berry College when Henry Ford unexpectedly showed up with a seven-piece orchestra. Compromise, however, is not always in the nature of individuals whose work calls for high doses of tenacity and drive; and it often must have been a bitter pill to swallow.

Some of the compromising extended into the curriculum, an area where battles raged over industrial versus academic training in general, but especially concerning African American uplift. The female school founders generally started with a curriculum that was familiar to them. They adjusted it somewhat to accommodate the realities of teacher availability. They then adjusted it further to accommodate the realities of potential financial support. Soon, the institution builders learned to be less tenacious about the details of what was learned than they were about the setting in which it was learned. Student behavior, rules about socializing across the sexes, dress codes, and general discipline were among the most important issues. The curriculum was subject to adjustment, which was subject to numerous variables.

The very authoritarian, even paternalistic, themes of these institutions may have reflected founders' desires for some control, some imprint that was not the artifact of compromise. In many instances, rules relating to students and their conduct were the only areas left where founders really could exercise nearly complete control, softening the reality of multiple compromises made to achieve institutional development and survival.

CHAPTER FOUR

Vocationalists: Education and Employability

A number of women who became southern educational leaders during the Progressive Era made their mark in improved opportunities and methods of vocational education. Their chosen niche is hardly surprising at a time when the concept of differentiated curriculum and the notion of industrial training in secondary schools found favor with many educators and policymakers, North and South.

Educational analysts often have noted darker motives concerning class and race distinctions in initiatives toward industrial training; and, indeed, compelling evidence exists for stalled general educational opportunities that have widened the gap between haves and have nots.[1] However, an examination of the work of southern women whose reform efforts were located in vocational education indicates that they were too savvy about outside influence and too committed to positive results to have misunderstood the potential of their cause. That cause, quite simply, focused on providing competencies that would open doors to personal economic stability—essential elements for economic and/or racial uplift. Sometimes basic elementary or early secondary education paved the way. At the other end of the spectrum, vocational schools sometimes grew to include liberal education. They generally also added large doses of morality and erally also added large doses of morality and spirituality. The women forging paths for industrial education, however, managed to incorporate multiple curricular elements without losing sight of employability. They incorporated into various aspects of their work a great deal of outspoken activism in support of gender and racial equity.

Typically, the southern educators who could be categorized as "vocationalists" were African Americans whose educational philosophies appeared in concert with those of Booker T. Washington and others who promoted economic uplift through job opportunities in those few areas then open to African Americans. This narrow arena included missionary and religious work, teaching, small business ownership, and other professions operating among African Americans. It also accounted for industrial workers, household workers, and a range of other semi-skilled and unskilled laborers. The vocationalist concept of uplift recognized that many young people subjected to dire socioeconomic circumstances and institutionalized racism had been afforded no opportunity to prepare for employment requiring even the most limited abilities. Educational endeavors embedded in this concept often started with basic literacy training and moved on to specific competencies for jobs that might range from laundress to bookkeeper and from Pullman porter to printer. The underlying impulse of educational reform in vocationalist terms was toward first steps for the neediest individuals, rather than toward the grander progressive aims of George Count's new social order or John Dewey's education for democracy. Nor did vocational education proponents claim that their approach supported general education, a deviation from the assertions of early proponents of manual training.[2]

Women categorized as vocationalists for purposes of this study founded educational institutions aimed at filling the gap between no opportunity and entry opportunity. However, a number of such educators—for example, Mary McLeod Bethune—deviated from the Booker T. Washington's accommodations when they added college-level general education to their agendas. Charlotte Hawkins Brown, although categorized in this study as a "collegian," could be viewed as a "vocationalist" if her own background and her long-term intentions for Palmer Institute were not taken into account. In practice, there was a thin line between educators who emphasized vocational skills while including some foundational Latin and literature and those who focused on collegiate education while casting a safety net toward at least some skill and semi-skill training.

Another example of deviation from the Washington model derives from the work of women educators outside the classroom or the campus. Typically, these African American women did not accommodate or compromise in their determination to visibly and vocally push for immediate and full inclusion of black citizens in all benefits of a democratic society. Risking the good will of some of their white northern benefactors, a number of the prominent female vocationalists spoke out vehemently and often for an end to racial and gender inequality. Nannie Helen Burroughs, who founded and led National Training School for Women and Girls in Washington, DC, also worked tirelessly for African Americans in her role as founder and then secretary of the Women's Auxiliary of the National Baptist Convention, as president of the National Association of Wage Earners, and as activist in antilynching crusades and black housing issues. Mary McLeod Bethune, deservedly revered for establishing the college that bears her name, is equally well regarded for her leadership of the National Association of Colored Women, the National Youth Administration, and the Association for the Study of Negro Life and History, as well as her close ties to President and Mrs. Franklin Roosevelt. Another vocational pioneer, Janie Porter Barrett, founded the Industrial Home School for Delinquent Colored Girls in Hanover County, VA, in 1915 and served as its superintendent for 25 years. She also gained prominence in the struggle for racial equality as the first president of the Virginia State Federation of Colored

Women's Clubs and a board member of the Richmond Urban League and the National Association of Colored Women.[3]

More typically in the South than elsewhere, educators concerned with social and economic uplift rarely veered far from religious and moral underpinnings in the curriculum. Their faith was abiding, their morality puritanical. The organized church, especially its missionary arms, was both a vessel to draw from—sometimes materially—and a vessel to fill. Church was community in the Progressive Era South, and founders of educational institutions worked with and through it, while embedding Christian tenets into the curriculum. Thus, when Mary McLeod Bethune conceptualized her educational efforts as a head, heart, and hand approach, she was emphasizing "Christianity, job training, and the mastery of at least elementary school subjects."[4] Denominational conventions, church women's groups, and missionary societies were major sources of support for institutions founded by women who directed their students to embrace, in fact intertwine, a Christian life and a learned vocation. Thus, morality and spirituality were both compelling ends and effective means for many industrial school operations.

The three women presented here as examples of commitment to vocational education in the Progressive Era—Nannie Helen Burroughs, Mary McLeod Bethune, and Elizabeth Evelyn Wright—were all school founders who demonstrated varied approaches within several central themes. Those themes include not only religious and moral betterment, but also service, racial uplift, and economic opportunity through employability. Perhaps more than most educational institutions since, the colleges founded by these women adopted from the start unequivocal goals and unambiguous methods. It is to the credit of their founders and their founding visions that all three survived the Depression and that two of the three have continued to thrive into the twenty-first century.

Nannie Helen Burroughs and a School For African American Females

When Jennie Poindexter Burroughs moved with her five-year-old daughter from rural Orange, Virginia, to Washington, DC, in 1884, possibilities became apparent. Large schools, government agencies, businesses run by and for African Americans, and a white upper class needing black labor marked hope for a widowed mother who was born a slave. Importantly, although the nation's capital was considered a southern town, the segregated public school system did not suffer the extremes of funding inequities well known in school systems elsewhere in the South. While Jennie Burroughs worked as a domestic servant, her daughter Nannie Helen Burroughs worked toward a different kind of life by attending the rigorous and well-regarded M Street High School.[5]

M Street was noted for pedagogy that emphasized critical thought over memorization and for a curriculum that offered languages and literature as well as literacy and industrial subjects. A four-year high school, it was unusual among public schools in the South for its ability to fully prepare African American students for higher education or for vocations. Nannie Helen Burroughs studied business and domestic science. Anticipating her later role as an educational leader, she founded the Harriet Beecher Stowe Literary Society which gave its members practice in writing and public speaking. A string of notable educators guided M Street High School at various times, including Francis L. Cardozo during Burroughs's attendance. Anna Julia Cooper, an activist for women's and African American causes and one of the first African American women to receive a B.A. degree (from Oberlin College, 1884), taught Latin at M Street and later became its principal.

Upon graduation from high school with honors in 1896, Burroughs badly wanted to find employment as a teaching assistant, or perhaps a teacher, in the Washington, DC, public schools. She later recalled that when she realized she couldn't manage to secure a teaching job, "It broke me up at first. I had all my life planned out, to settle down in Washington with my mother, do that pleasant work...."[6] Race and lack of social connection undoubtedly contributed to her initially stalled career.

The remaining likely alternative for an African American female seeking gainful employment was domestic service. However, the woman who would spend most of the rest of her life increasing career options for others decided she must find something else for herself. Fortunately, Burroughs was willing to be geographically mobile; equally fortunately, she was a dedicated Baptist with strong religious and community ties to the Baptist church. This combination eventually led to another job choice for her, and she became associate editor of *The Christian Banner*, a Baptist newspaper with offices in Philadelphia, PA. Within a few years, she moved back to Washington, DC, where her mother and several other relatives still lived. Again, Burroughs was thwarted in her job search. After scoring high marks on the civil service examination, she sought a position as a government clerk but was told the only available openings were for white clerks. Once more, she turned to the Baptist network, taking a job as bookkeeper and editorial secretary to the Foreign Mission Board of the National Baptist Convention. The Board moved its offices to Louisville, KY, in 1900, and Burroughs relocated to keep her job.[7]

Like many other women born and raised in the South who gravitated to educational reform efforts, Nannie Helen Burroughs would translate her own experiences into a single-case needs assessment and a mandate to plan for change through education. Her most vivid firsthand knowledge centered around lack of appropriate job opportunities for African American females. Her response reflected her determination that the problem was lodged not only in systemic inequities but also in individual inadequacies, including lack of appropriate job skills, limited ability in self-presentation, and unrealistic understanding of the nature of the marketplace. So strong was Burroughs's commitment to skill building for women that while in Louisville she founded a women's club that offered evening classes in typing, bookkeeping, sewing, and cooking.[8]

Burroughs's general ideas for increased opportunities for African American women took a first step toward reality when she was invited to speak at the 1900 annual conference of the National Baptist Convention in Richmond, VA. Already a noted speaker at local church events, she quickly soared to national prominence with eloquent oratory in a presentation about the issue of limiting women's church involvement titled "Hindered from Helping." The male-dominated National Baptist Convention, long reluctant to allow a unit for women, now voted to establish a Woman's Convention. Burroughs, at 21 years old, was elected corresponding secretary of the Woman's Convention, a position which she quickly expanded to include nationwide fund raising and public relations. Her success in raising money for missionary work and raising membership through mail campaigns and stump speeches netted her a salary for what was originally to be an upaid position.[9]

At the first meeting of the Woman's Convention, in 1901, Burroughs proposed a "National Training School" for women. The proposal languished in the decision-making process until a vote in 1904 to accept her recommendation and begin to secure funding for the school. Burroughs, persistent in her desire to garner support for her idea, claimed there was "no movement so essential at this period of our religious development as a denomination and as a race."[10] In a politically savvy maneuver, she emphasized to her fellow Baptist women the benefits of the proposed school to missionary work, insisting that it would provide consistent training to missionary women from Africa and other countries, as well as women throughout the United States. Additional subject training was mentioned, but in a position somewhat subordinate to missionary work, in Burrough's 1904 appeal to the group:

> We need an institution where women from all parts of the country may come and receive first-class training for Missionary, Sunday School and Church Work, as well as training in all the household arts, such as cooking, sewing, housekeeping, nursing and as much of the theory of horticulture as we can possibly give. We have no specific home mission work before us and there are hundreds of dollars that can be secured for this and for no other purpose.... Other denominations and organizations are preparing men and women to fill positions of every conceivable kind and it is but in keeping with the progressive missionary spirit of the hour that every denomination have its own trained workers.[11]

More than many school and college founders, Burroughs was positioned to hit the ground running with her plans to build an institution. Through an assignment that provided travel and contacts and through personal abilities to mobilize others, she had already built a base of support among an auxiliary group of Baptist women and garnered at least some sanction for that base among the Baptist men who controlled the National Baptist Convention. Unlike many of her counterparts in southern educational reform, she was quickly supported in her efforts by a large, grassroots network comprised largely of ministers' wives and other women active in local church organizations. Similar to many of her counterparts, however, Burroughs was tenacious in maximizing each small advantage that would move her closer to her objective. In this regard, she interpreted her role as corresponding secretary of the Woman's Convention broadly. Where she might have merely mailed out meeting minutes, she instead sent ideas for projects and appeals for funds. Where she might have simply reported events from the field, she pushed women to support women. Her very first correspondence solicited donations to send a female missionary to Africa, which soon arrived in amounts well above expectations. She noted that "with a united sisterhood our educational, home and foreign mission work will receive new impetus."[12]

By contemporary standards, Burroughs would be perceived as strictly antifeminist. Her original agenda for the National Training School was fourfold: to train women for foreign missionary work, to prepare women for religious teaching in Sunday schools, to train women as better homemakers, and to qualify women for employment in domestic service.[13] Indeed, even though the school would quickly add training in secretarial practices, millinery and dressmaking skills, and music, its purpose was embedded in the tightly circumscribed range of possibilities for African American women early in the twentieth century. Burroughs's own frustration at graduating from high school to confront multiple closed doors in her search for employment may have played a part in her decision to guide young women toward opportunities that were realistic in a world of limited possibilities. She later explained:

> An idea stuck out from the suffering of that disappointment that I would some day have a school here in Washington that school politics had nothing to do with, and that would give all sorts of girls a fair chance, without political pull, to help them overcome whatever handicaps they might have.[14]

In an early publicity flyer for the school, Burroughs noted, "Thousands of young women are turned out to make their way in the world every year, and they constitute a class of "make shifts." Many of them want to do better and will do better if properly trained."[15]

Burroughs guided a subcommittee of the Woman's Convention charged with site selection for the school, and by 1906 the women found a dilapidated eight-room farm house on a hill in "Lincoln Heights," an unimproved neighborhood in southeast Washington, DC. Situated on six acres, in an area with no streets, phone service, or electricity, the property also had a barn, a stable, a well, and a panoramic view. Burroughs, undaunted by the $6,000 price tag, went back to Louisville to quickly raise the $500 down payment from the church people she knew best. In January 1907, Burroughs and two other members of the site selection subcommittee incorporated the National Training School for Women and Girls.[16]

After two years spent forming a local committee of interested church women, raising funds to pay the remainder of the property purchase price, and recruiting students and staff, the National Training School opened in 1909 with seven students who fit the requirement that they qualify for matriculation at the high school or junior college level. By the end of the year, 32 students attended classes in mission work, academics, sewing, and music. Burroughs, elected president of the school by its board of trustees, raised enough new money during the year to begin plans for a building program that would eventually encompass nine structures. These included classroom buildings, a trades practice building, dormitories, a chapel, and an administration building.[17]

Spiritual and moral uplift, discipline, and attention to personal hygiene were part of Burroughs's conservative creed for the students. She labeled her theme for the development of young women "the three Bs--Bible, bath, and broom." Students were to adhere to Christian life tenets, personal cleanliness, and excellent homemaking. They attended chapel daily, worked in campus jobs, left campus only when chaperoned, and subjected their correspondence and packages to inspection. One of several school mottos was, "Wherever you live, make that place better." Others were, "We specialize in the impossible" and "Learn to do one thing superbly well." Later, Burroughs opened a commercial laundry at the school to teach laundering, assist needy student workers, and save money on school laundry. Its motto was "Learn to earn and earn to learn."[18]

The curriculum of the school grew and changed substantially during its first several decades of existence, although it remained primarily vocational in intent. The seven original departments (missionary, music, dressmaking and millinery, laundry, business, domestic science, and Sunday school teaching) transformed into a group of program areas that included trade programs (including nursing, social service, beauty culture, printing, and others), academic programs (with junior high school level preparatory students), and teacher training. After two decades, the school had enrolled more than 2,000 students from 40 states, Africa, Central America, Haiti, and Puerto Rico. Burroughs applauded its position as the only boarding school of African American girls north of Richmond.

Burroughs was very much in the Booker T. Washington tradition with regard to the virtues of labor, especially the professionalization of labor that could offer possibilities in a limited African American job market. "Don't scorn labor nor look with contempt upon the laborer," she warned. The school changed its name twice, both times retaining the vocationalist spirit—first as the National Seminary and Trade School for Women and Girls and then as the National Trade and Professional School for Women and Girls. Burroughs saw domestic service as a particularly worthy calling, as it could provide an income for women working outside the home or improve the quality of life for full time homemakers. Homemaking for Burroughs encompassed almost every trade, from laundering to tailoring. "The greatest unmet educational need of the Negro race is for women with trained heads, hands and hearts to develop the social and esthetic taste of its home and church life," she insisted. "The Negro home is in dire need of transformation. It is woefully lacking in applied ideals and atmosphere."[19]

Like her counterparts in other private school endeavors, fund-raising acumen was crucial to Burroughs's efforts. Never married and never a mother, she had time and energy to attend to the school's survival almost single-handedly. The Woman's Convention, which grew to nearly a million members by 1920, donated small amounts fairly regularly and provided a fund-raising base. Burroughs's tenacity and skill in public speaking and mail campaigns did the rest. She was highly organized in her presentations, prepared to demonstrate exactly what the school was doing and exactly what the funds would accomplish-- generally facilities, facility improvements, and student support. Several large foundations, such as Phelps-Stokes and Slater funds, contributed to the school, along with church groups, women's clubs, and individual donors. However, the school was never dependent on northern white philanthropy. Additional support came from entrepreneurial ideas, such as the public laundry and a working print shop on the school premises. Burroughs hosted a concert at which the Hampton Institute choir performed and staged plays by her students. In 1933, she campaigned to collect a million coupons from Colgate products toward a $4,000 prize. The same year, amidst the desperation of the Depression, Burroughs staged a "pantry shower" that brought donations of groceries to the school from churches and clubs up and down the East Coast. In the trades building, students were busy making "barrel chairs" to sell to the general public. These were fashioned by slicing the upper front off a wooden barrel, adding a seat, cushioning the back and seat, and placing a skirt around the bottom.[20]

Through political activism in causes like antilynching and African American housing, as well as her work for the Republican National Committee during several presidential campaigns, Burroughs made friends with other influential African Americans who were able to productively lend their support to the school. Carter Woodson, for example, wrote in the Baltimore paper, *The Afro American*, a long article that applauded the practical curriculum, the professionalism of the graduates, and Burroughs herself:

> At the National Training School, Nannie Burroughs is doing a work which neither the public schools nor the university can do. The other schools have their spheres and the National Training School has its special sphere. In the large school systems teachers are merely parts of a machine and they teach books; but in Miss Burroughs' school the instructors teach the students--actually educate them by bringing out into action the powers of the mind. ...I am giving this school one hundred dollars this year. How much will you give?[21]

Not entirely unexpectedly, the stubborn tenacity that enabled Burroughs to build a school could aggravate some who were key to the school's success. Typically, those less friendly to the school felt it was too tightly controlled by the woman at its helm. In the case of the men in the National Baptist Convention, the success of the school and their inability to control it paved the way for a protracted takeover attempt. The first salvo in the ongoing battles between Burroughs and the National Baptist Convention came in 1916 after the Convention split and the new National Baptist Convention, U.S.A., sought to consolidate all its board and auxiliaries under tight control. Its new charter stated that "auxiliary Boards and their officers and directors shall have and exercise no power of control over the affairs and properties of said Boards independent of this corporation," and demanded the auxiliary elements amend their own charters to show "they are under and subject to the jurisdiction and control of this corporation."[22]

Burroughs insisted that the Woman's Convention should continue its relative independence and that the school was under the jurisdiction of its board of trustees, an 80-member self-perpetuating board of women from state Baptist conventions throughout the country. The trustees, highly satisfied with Burroughs's work, held tightly to the position that they were the legal custodians of the school and refused to turn the property over to the National Baptist Convention. With other pressing matters and leadership changes, the National Baptist Convention allowed the matter to drift as unfinished business for several years, until 1924, when president L. K. Williams from Texas again took up the cause. He managed to find some support among Woman's Convention membership, but could not split the Board of Trustees. Typically, Burroughs attended annual conferences to vocally and vehemently argue, accuse, and stall with regard to the men who wanted to take over the school. She saw the ongoing determination for strictly male control of all things Baptist as an indication of enormous problems that would occur if the all female school were taken over by the men.[23] In a 1938 statement she made as corresponding secretary, she railed against the widening control of the men:

> The members of the Boards of the National Baptist Convention have membership in the National Baptist Convention and have equal participation in all functions of the convention. Members of the Woman's

> Convention do not have any such rights in the National Baptist Convention....At present the Woman's convention is legally and directly under a Board of Directors of the National Baptist Convention made up entirely of men. This is not only undemocratic and reactionary, but manifestly unfair in this day when Negro women are carrying almost the entire burden in our churches.[24]

The same year, the National Baptist Convention board of directors resolved to "withdraw all connections, allegiance, and support" from the school.[25] The Woman's Convention, however, continued its support for the school and eventually reaffirmed its support of Burroughs by electing her to its presidency in 1949. She served in that capacity until her death in 1961.

Whatever fighting spirit Burroughs did not completely expend on the school, she applied to the struggle for African American rights and betterment. Her cutting edge efforts in this arena included a 1902 written appeal to a white women's group seeking their support for equal treatment of blacks in public transportation and a 1915 speech urging Washington, DC, blacks to boycott buses in protest of their relegation to seats in the back.[26] Later, Burroughs became an activist in antilynching crusades, founder and president of the National Association of Wage Earners, a founder of the International Council of Women of the Darker Races of the World, and president of the National League of Republican Colored Women (whose officers also included Charlotte Hawkins Brown and Mary Church Terrell).

In her social reform work, Burroughs was impatient not only with whites who withheld equal opportunities, but also with those African Americans whose behavior amounted to tacit acquiescence with racism or lack of effort in bettering themselves. Her small monograph, *Think on These Things,* contained a list of "Twelve Things the Negro Must Do for Himself and Twelve Things the White Man Must Stop Doing to the Negro" that indicted both races for the closed doors and limited opportunities experienced by African Americans.[27]

Increased opportunities for black citizens to participate in public secondary education meant some reduced interest in the National Trade and Professional School for Women and Girls during the second half of the twentieth century. By 1956, only a summer institute remained open. In 1964, however, the school was renamed the Nannie Helen Burroughs School and revised as a kindergarten through grade six school with a Christian environment. The school property was transferred to the ownership of the Progressive National Baptist Convention.

Fiery and focused, Burroughs was later aptly characterized by her friend and early biographer Earl Harrison as "courageous, charming, and dynamic to the point that she was irresistible to the open minded and contemptible to the jealous and prejudiced."[28]

Mary McLeod Bethune and Triumphs of the Heart

The similarities and dissimilarities in the early lives and works of women like Nannie Helen Burroughs and Mary McLeod Bethune tell an intriguing tale of multiple routes plotted in widely scattered endeavors toward southern educational betterment in the Progressive Era. The stories of African American educators in particular also demarcate a path of educational change that started humbly with freed blacks and mission schooling in Union controlled areas of the South even slightly before the final curtain on slavery at Appomattox. Reconstruction and subsequent years brought a wave of Freedmen's Bureau, American Missionary Association, and other educational activity supported by–especially in the industrial training arena–white philanthropy from the North. In a few areas, support even grew for public schooling of black citizens. The black women of the South who were positioned to initiate Progressive Era educational reforms represented the first generation to have fully participated in these struggling post-Civil War educational opportunities. The multiplier effect slowly at work through the efforts of some of the most talented and tenacious among them demonstrated the reaches of possibility for future advancement.

Among the many influential women born into the uneasy postwar freedom from slavery, Mary McLeod Bethune would eventually stand out as a beacon for African Americans who held dear the ideal of full participation in the opportunities of a democracy and who understood that education was an essential component of that dream. Her early narrative history, a compelling and heart-warming tale of toil and triumph, largely has been derived from her own recollections and friendly biographers. Although undoubtedly embellished when it was convenient to offer audiences a dramatic boot-strapping story, the contextual reality of time and place leaves reason to conclude that at least the essential elements, if not the anecdotal details, of Bethune's self-reported biography are as close to accurate as memory could manage.[29]

"I could see little white boys and girls going to school every day, learning to read and write, living in comfortable homes," recalled Bethune, born in 1875 in Mayesville, SC, the fifteenth of seventeen children of Samuel and Patsy McLeod, former slaves turned scratch cotton farmers. "I was with no opportunity, no chance to grow. I found myself very often yearning all along for the things that were being provided for the white children with whom I had to chop cotton every day, or pick up corn, or whatever the task happened to be. I think that actually the first hurt that came to me in my childhood was the contrast of what was being done for the white children and the lack of what we got."[30]

The McLeod family experienced in rural South Carolina what amounted to a somewhat typical life for communities of freed slaves. Mary Jane's mother and father, talented and tenacious, managed to scrape together enough barter and cash for a small cotton patch and to build by hand a small, windowless cabin. While pursuing the life of freed slaves after the Civil War, they gathered back together those of Mary Jane's older brothers and sisters who had been enslaved at different plantations in the area.

All children who could walk worked on the small family farm or as day laborers at nearby plantations.

Mary Jane McLeod formed at this early stage in her life the idea that African American women were the key to all manner of reform for their race. She viewed family environment as a determining force in every human life and observed that the nature of that environment was indelibly shaped by the matriarch. Her own mother, by family lore descended from African royalty, had continued to cook for her former master after the Civil War, saving enough from her earnings as a free woman to purchase five acres of land from him that would be the start of a family farm. Bethune would later describe Patsy McLeod as a woman who, although illiterate, had "great vision. She had a great understanding of human nature...a great philosophy of life." While her father was "very kindly disposed, very sympathetic," her mother possessed the "willpower and drive that held our household together."[31]

Bethune also recalled her mother as a "master of all the home arts" who had learned and practiced the manner and speech of the cultivated white people who had owned her. "You would have thought if you talked with her she was an educated person. [She] showed very little sign of ignorance.... She was jolly, but firm–the great educator." Her father, on the other hand, "did not have my mother's fire in him....He caught onto things quickly and cooperated with my mother." Called "Aunt Patsy" by friends and neighbors, Patsy McLeod took on the informal role of community midwife, nurse, and social worker. Bethune credited that example as her role model for the importance of service.[32]

Operationalizing the ideal of women as African American role models started with their placement in the family and extended to their placement in African American uplift ideology. Women like Bethune, Mary Church Terrell, Charlotte Hawkins Brown, and Anna Julia Cooper proved to be as noteworthy in the struggle for black educational opportunity as Booker T. Washington and W.E.B. DuBois. Bethune, in particular, never veered far from the notion that racial uplift started with strong families, and strong families were the responsibilities of strong mothers. "Next to God, we are indebted to women," she maintained, "first for life itself, and then for making it worth having."[33]

Given her acknowledgment of matriarchal prominence and importance, Bethune found it pragmatic, and not antifeminist, to include training in domestic arts as essential curricular fare at the school for women that she would eventually nudge into existence. In 1926, Bethune declared a philosophy of education for the females of her race that delineates a critical conundrum of her thought and work: What appears to be gender pigeonholing in present perspective may have been practical wisdom in the early twentieth-century southern context:

> If there is to be any distinctive difference between the education of the Negro girl and the Negro boy, it should be that of consideration for the unique responsibility of this girl in the world today. The challenge to the Negro home is one which dares the Negro to develop initiative to solve his own problems, to work out his own problems, to work out his difficulties in a superior fashion, and to finally come into his right as an American Citizen, because he is tolerated. This is the moral responsibility of the education of the Negro girl.... Such is the natural endowment which her education must make it possible for her to bequeath to the future the Negro race. The education of the Negro girl must embrace a larger appreciation for good citizenship in the home. Our girls must be taught cleanliness, beauty and thoughtfulness and their application in making home life possible.[34]

By the time she was out of her teens, Mary Jane McLeod would be able to credit several additional female role models who introduced her to formal education, especially in the areas of religious and vocational training, and who would have a profound effect on the educational philosophies that she eventually would embrace for her own work. The first of these, Emma Jane Wilson, arrived from her hometown of Manning, SC, to open Trinity Presbyterian Mission School in 1885, about five miles from the McLeod cabin. Thrilled to be allowed to attend, and especially to have the chance to learn to read and write, young Mary gladly made the ten-mile walk each day of the school session and in turn taught literacy at home to a number of her siblings. Wilson recognized a bright future in her young pupil and nominated Mary Jane McLeod for a scholarship provided by Mary Chrissman, a Quaker teacher in Colorado who had saved her extra earnings from seamstress work in order to send a deserving child to further schooling. The scholarship enabled Bethune an excellent opportunity to further her education at Scotia Seminary for Negro Girls (which later became Barber-Scotia College), Emma Wilson's alma mater, in Concord, NC. From 1888 to 1894, Bethune worked through a multifaceted curriculum which included liberal arts, domestic and industrial arts, Christian-centered religious training, and music. Surrounded by serious female students preparing for lives of leadership and service, Bethune undoubtedly learned something about the power of educated womanhood.[35]

During her last year at Scotia, Bethune sent an application to the Bible Institute for Home and Foreign Missions, an interdenominational evangelical missionary training school in Chicago that later became Moody Bible Institute. When she was accepted, Mary Chrissman again helped with necessary costs. Decidedly proselytizing in purpose, the Institute emphasized learning to spread the Christian word by practicing to spread the Christian word. Students fanned into the soup kitchens, police lock-ups, and tenements of Chicago to spread the message of faith and invite the urban poor to religious services at the Institute. Bethune, the only African American student at the time, was quickly selected as a soloist for the Institute's performing choir. This experience included participation on the "Gospel Car," a train car full of singers and workers who would travel to Iowa, Nebraska, and the Dakotas to share the Christian gospel and establish Sunday schools. Mary Jane McLeod was frequently the first African American the children of the northern Midwest had seen; and by the time the trip ended, she was well schooled in fielding pointed questions about her color as well as in the activities of an evangelical missionary. She was ready to fulfill her dream of becoming a missionary in Africa, and she applied to the Mission Board of the Presbyterian Church for an appointment. In a turn of events that marked a great personal disappointment, she was informed there were no positions for African Americans.

This unhappy news eventually led Bethune on another formative path and into the arena of influence of an important new mentor, Lucy Craft Laney. With foreign missionary work blocked, Bethune sought the next apparent route toward serving her people—teaching. Still working through the Presbyterian Mission Board, she first moved back home and became an assistant to Emma Wilson at her Mayesville school. A year later, she was transferred by the Mission Board to the Haines Industrial Institute, Augusta, GA, a model of schooling for African Americans that had been founded in 1883 by the exceedingly well, educated and visionary African American Lucy Craft Laney.

Although Laney was born in Georgia in 1854, well before emancipation, her father, a master carpenter and Presbyterian preacher, had already managed to purchase his own and her mother's freedom. Lucy Laney, with help from the family that had once owned her mother, graduated from Atlanta University and then attended the University of Chicago. She then worked as a teacher in the Georgia towns of Milledgeville, Macon, Augusta, and Savannah. Her decision to open a mission school for black children in Augusta was made with an impulse toward the service ideal, racial uplift, and religious zeal. Encouraged and at least morally supported by the Presbyterian Board of Missions, the school that started with five children in a church basement in 1883 grew to 234 students the following year. Francine Haines, an early benefactor and officer in Presbyterian women's clubs, provided the name for the school as it grew to nearly 1,000 students and 30 teachers by 1915. The Haines Institute was noted for teacher training, a nursing program, other vocational training, and some liberal arts—a blend that spelled for Laney the range of options necessary for racial uplift.[36]

The year that Mary McLeod Bethune spent at Haines Institute undoubtedly taught her a great deal about institution building. Lucy Craft Laney could be observed as a superb teacher; a master negotiator of the politics of fund raising; and a determined proponent of the notion that women, in their roles as teachers and homemakers, were the key to improving opportunities and conditions for black Americans. Bethune later recalled, "Lucy Laney with her spirit of service, quick steps, determination, will, alert mind, again demonstrated to me that it could be done. I studied her, watched her every move and gave myself full to the cause she represented."[37]

While much of the Haines Institute curriculum appeared inspired by Booker T. Washington, W.E.B. DuBois praised her as the single individual who "kept the fires of Negro education fiercely flaming in the rich but mean-spirited city of Augusta, Georgia."[38] Bethune, who readily named Laney as one of her most important mentors and role models, was in a position to observe firsthand the delicate interweaving of academic preparation, industrial training, religious emphasis, strict discipline, and racial pride. Although Haines was a co-educational school, Laney's belief in the power of black womanhood probably served to articulate and reinforce Bethune's own developing philosophies.

After a year at Haines, the Presbyterian Mission Board moved Bethune back to South Carolina, where she taught at the Kendall Institute in Sumter and met Albertus Bethune, a retail salesman, who she would marry in 1897. Their son, Albert, was born a year later while they were living in Savannah, GA. By 1899, Bethune was ready to return to teaching and found a Presbyterian mission position in the small village of Palatka, FL, where she established a school as part of the local Presbyterian church. However needy, Palatka had little potential for fostering an educational institution that might grow to any size. Bethune soon found herself looking to other areas of Florida for opportunities to serve black citizens while building a school that might become stable and even thrive. Daytona, a popular Atlantic coast vacation and second home spot for wealthy northerners, as well as home to a large and poor black population, seemed particularly appropriate. In the first decade of the twentieth century, its population of about 2,000 was 50 percent African American. It is unclear how Bethune's desire to follow her calling might have been greeted by Albertus Bethune, and little is know about his activities during the early years in Daytona, but the couple stayed together for only about a year or two after their arrival in Daytona in 1904. However, they remained legally married until Albertus Bethune's death in 1918.

Daytona would prove a wise choice for its confluence of black citizens neglected by the public education system and wealthy white visitors with funds to spare for good works. Mary McLeod Bethune played the role of matchmaker between the two groups by starting a school that demonstrated needs and possibilities and by tenaciously and eloquently garnering the funding that would assure the school's growth into a significant educational institution for thousands of African Americans. With the $1.50 she had in her pocket by the time she moved to Daytona, she talked her way into an advance for rental on a five-room cottage where she lived and where she welcomed five young girls to the Daytona Educational and Industrial Training School for Negro Girls in October 1904. Bethune maintained,

> The aim of the institution is to uplift Negro girls spiritually, morally, intellectually and industrially. The school stands for a broad, thorough practical training. To develop Christian character, to send forth women who will be well-rounded home-makers and Christian leaders is the aim of its founder and supporters, a trained mind, heart and hand being their idea of a complete education.[39]

As the community got word of the school, it began to outgrow its location and its funding. Early donations were in-kind contributions of dishes, furniture, and food, often in response to Bethune's solicitations as she rode through the neighborhood on her second-hand bicycle. Church groups and local clubs began to take notice and could be counted on to help with ongoing necessities. Within a few years, Bethune selected and managed to purchase a larger site for the school; and she and her students worked tirelessly to clear it of trash that had accumulated during the years the community had used that lot as a local dump. The first building, constructed in a stop-and-start manner that fit the vagaries of available funds, was a multipurpose, four-story clapboard dwelling named "Faith Hall" after the main building at Scotia Seminary. Although the unfinished interior had no plaster and only ladders for stairs, Bethune relocated her school to Faith Hall, on the current Bethune-Cookman College property, in 1907. She formed a board of trustees, hired Hunter College graduate and experienced educator Frances Keyser, and set about institution building in earnest.

The curriculum of Bethune's school quickly evolved toward high school level education, but never veered from its commitment to vocational training and religion across the curriculum. The three-pronged concept of head, heart, and hand described the underlying rationale for coursework which, by 1910, encompassed an English Department, an Industrial Department, and a Biblical Department. Bethune was particularly insistent that the religious training be more than just a glorified Sunday school. Bible instruction was included every day, as were two quiet periods a day for Bible study. The religious spirit, Bethune maintained, "must pervade all of the curriculum. The life of the institution must be saturated [with it]; it should well up in the instructors; it must be written into the very purposes of the school itself....In founding my college, for example, our motivation was religious; we had set before us the ideal of a whole school for Christian service."[40]

The vocational education of the school—the "hand" portion of the three-pronged educational approach—initially centered on domestic arts and home crafts. After the move to a permanent location, Bethune added a school farm for self-sustenance and learning, including pigs donated by Booker T. Washington, a Jersey milk cow, chickens, a sugar cane crop, and ample fruits and vegetables. Eventually, the vocational fare expanded toward professional areas, with emphases in teacher training and nursing education.[41]

Wise and fortunate in the chosen location of her school, Bethune was quick to begin to meet potential northern benefactors. The first of those who would help assure the survival of the endeavor was James Gamble, philanthropist son of the founder of Proctor & Gamble, Inc., who owned a winter home in Daytona. When the school had been in operation less than a year and had twenty students, Bethune wrote him a note asking for an appointment, rode her bicycle to his home, and during their first meeting asked him to become a trustee. Undoubtedly influenced by Bethune's dignified and persuasive presence, as well as the school's clear need, he accepted and became the first chairman of the board of trustees. Others who joined the board were two ministers of local African American churches, the mayor of Daytona, and a well-known realtor. They managed to open doors for Bethune, including those of local hotels. At the Howard, the Hamilton, the Ormond, and the Palmetto hats were passed after choral groups from the school performed in the lobbies or out on the front verandahs. Importantly, these entertainments sparked many long-term benefactor relationships. For example, sewing machine and auto manufacturer Thomas White visited the school after hearing the girls sing at the Palmetto. He made regular visits and contributions to the school for many years after, frequently visiting Bethune during his winter vacations from Cleveland, Ohio. Another winter resident, George S. Doane, could be counted on as a frequent donor, as could Louise Ferris Meigs, daughter of the benefactor of Sarah Lawrence College. A group of wealthy women who had formed Daytona's Palmetto Club also became a source of ongoing support. In a small beach town that swelled with wealthy vacationers each winter, it was relatively easy to attract the attention of potential friends and benefactors. Many well-off northerners undoubtedly felt as Thomas White did when he wrote in the school's guest book during his first visit, "This is the most heart-warming thing I have seen in Florida."[42]

The school grew to include more students in more grades and to boast a nearly $500,000 real estate value by the end of its second decade.[43] Bethune also managed eventually to garner funds from the Carnegie Foundation, General Education Board, the Slater Fund, and the Rosenwald Fund. Nevertheless, like other private schools serving populations that could afford only minimal tuition, the Daytona Industrial and Training School continually struggled to remain financially viable. After weighing a number of options for assuring permanent financial stability, Bethune and her board of trustees decided to affiliate the school with the Methodist Episcopal Church in 1923. This affiliation led to the school's eventual merger with Cookman Institute, a Methodist-supported school founded in Jacksonville, Florida, in 1872 and named for Methodist preacher Alfred Cookman.

The first institution of higher education for black students in the state, the coeducational Cookman Institute prepared students for teaching, missionary and ministry work, vocations, or further academic study at colleges and universities that accepted black students. Although the school had earned a fine reputation, it floundered after a devastating fire in 1915 and changes in leadership that followed. By 1923, the Methodist Episcopal Church began the process of merging the Daytona and Jacksonville schools, including plans for turning the Daytona campus into a coeducational setting. The school took the name Daytona-Cookman Collegiate Institute, and the first men's dormitory, Cookman Hall, was dedicated in 1925. Official documents listed Bethune as "founder and president." After several years of additional expansion, the coeducational school took the name it would have for the remainder of the twentieth century, Bethune-Cookman College.[44]

The transition to a coeducational institution was somewhat smoother than the transition to Methodist affiliation. Although the Methodists did help the Bethune-Cookman open doors to some valuable funding sources, the church was unable, especially during the Depression years, to meet financial support commitments outlined in its initial agreement with the school. This remained a disappointment to Bethune through her resignation as president in 1942. Bethune-Cookman continued to expand, however, largely fueled by growing funding from private sources, continuing interest from potential students, and increasing demands from the state of Florida for trained teachers for African American elementary school students. A junior college was added, and in 1931, Bethune-Cookman College was accredited by the Southern Association of Colleges and Secondary Schools. The junior college enrollment grew from 15 in 1927 to 197 in 1937. Although the school began to plan for closing its high school division and becoming a four-year college, vocational training in farming, mechanical and industrial arts, secretarial skills, and homemaking remained important throughout Bethune's presidency.[45]

During the 1930s, Bethune maintained her preference for the school's role in African American female uplift, urging that, "As a standard coeducational junior college Bethune-Cookman may be competent, but just another school. As a designed and inspired four-year college for Negro girls it can serve a unique function, one that cannot readily be served by other institutions."[46]

Like so many visionary and energetic African Americans of the early twentieth century, Bethune understood that her work in education was inextricably linked to larger local, national, and international issues related to race and class. Determined to serve in all those arenas, Bethune started early and started in her own backyard. For the children in labor camps that housed local turpentine workers five miles from her school, she founded Tomoka Mission and the Better Boys Club in an effort to bring education and general welfare to struggling black families. Starting in 1912, African American residents had a local hospital that would accept them as patients. Bethune founded McLeod Hospital as both a teaching site for nurses and a badly needed community service.[47]

It was Bethune's leadership in black women's clubs, however, that would eventually propel her to national prominence as an activist for African American and women's causes. Considering the location of African American women on the outermost fringes of democratic opportunity during the first half of the twentieth century, the trajectory of Bethune to the central core of national debate was a stunning achievement.

Elaine Smith, noting Bethune's "power organizing dynamic," credited several personal characteristics and competencies with launching her success in mobilizing organizations for service and activism: "her intense motivation, her passion for cohesiveness, and her bold vision and execution"[48]

Her knowledge of the local women's club arena began when she hosted meetings at the Daytona Institute. By 1917, she was the president of the Florida Federation of Colored Women's Clubs, a position she held for eight years. At Bethune's urging, the club took up the cause of young black women by founding a home for wayward and delinquent girls and by eventually convincing the Florida legislature to support it. Bethune also became president of the Florida State Teachers Association, the Southeastern Association of Colored Women, and, from 1924 to 1928, the National Association of Colored Women. In 1935, she organized and became president of the National Council of Negro Women, an umbrella group with the ideal of more clout than any single women's organization might achieve. Bethune, never veering far from her commitment to the future of young black women, stated at the organizational meeting, "We need an organization to open new doors for our young women and when the council speaks its power will be felt." She insisted that the new council "can make a stronger appeal for putting over big projects."[49]

Undoubtedly, the idea of "big projects" for the Council was sparked by President Roosevelt's promising New Deal programs, as well as by Bethune's disappointment that the National Association of Colored Women was more decentralized than she preferred and could not be counted on during difficult Depression years to assert influence in Washington. The National Council of Negro Women, however, was clearly dominated by Bethune's vision of a strong Washington presence to assert pressure on government actors, to increase visibility for various causes and issues, and to incorporate internationalism into its service and networking agenda. While a number of influential black women, including Mary Church Terrell and Charlotte Hawkins Brown, were initially skeptical that the Council was needed, Bethune singlehandedly turned the organization into an entity that government officials needed to reckon with concerning programs and policies influencing black citizens.[50]

Soon after, Bethune increased her opportunities to push for black participation in the fruits of the New Deal by accepting an appointment from President Roosevelt as director of the Division of Negro Affairs in the National Youth Administration, a post she held from 1936 to 1944. From that post, she was able to assure that thousands of black youths received a fair share of government-supported college funding, job training, and employment opportunities. She also became a respected and trusted friend of both President and Mrs. Roosevelt and was able to interpret for them and other high level federal officials the black situation and black needs.

Mary McLeod Bethune, at least by reputation, deviated from other tenacious women who built institutions from nearly nothing during the Progressive Era. Unlike Nannie Helen Burroughs, Charlotte Hawkins Brown, or Alice Lloyd, she had few, if any, real detractors. Her struggles with her board members, affiliate institutions, or others were minimal; and her personality was not abrasive or controlling. Yet her skill as a persuasive one-on-one or group tactician did not extend to pandering to individuals who could help her. She held her ground for the betterment of blacks and women with finesse and aplomb. Although in the early days of Bethune's school, a few black citizens in Daytona voiced objections concerning industrial training for African Americans while whites were being prepared for college, Bethune seemed able to largely defuse that sentiment.[51] Was she really that good, or has her history soared in the absence of a critical biography?

Audrey Thomas McCluskey examined the complexities of Bethune's reality and legacy to give an appropriate summation of her personal and political skill in moving individuals and organizations in directions that represented her own mission:

> Although she held fast to her core beliefs—including religious faith, racial pride, and equal opportunity for black women and men in America—she adjusted her approach, if not her values, to the existing climate as needed. Despite her limited education, she possessed an orator's command of the language....Bethune's complexities included her sophisticated political instincts, which came more from observation and practice than from reading and self-reflection; her staunch and unwavering patriotism; her strong sense of self in a society that demeaned and devalued people who looked like her.[52]

Elizabeth Evelyn Wright of Voorhees College

The stories of successful institutional fund-raising efforts, scattered with names of rich and famous northern benefactors and their philanthropic funds, are particularly intriguing for anecdotes about persistent women convincing powerful men to open their wallets for good causes. They also raise perplexing questions about the nature of inevitable compromises that pioneering educators needed to make in order to attract and keep their sources of funding.

However, the substantial northern philanthropic support of southern education largely has overshadowed the contributions of thousands of African Americans who gave at church when the plate was passed in the name of a new school, who sent their children to school with pennies and dimes for the teachers, and who contributed food and durable goods whenever possible. Anderson and Moss, writing about northern philanthropy to southern education during the first three decades of the twentieth century, note, "It is inaccurate to think of southern blacks as mere receivers of charity. Not only were northern donors often forced to take into account the educational goals of African Americans, but black communities were also donors, contributing millions of dollars in educational self-help." During the first 50 years following the Civil War and the emancipation of black slaves, northern philanthropy accounted for donations of $57 million to black educational institutions, while African American contributions amounted to $25 million.[53]

While there is no doubt that the larger and more prestigious institutions were those that benefited substantially from white northern philanthropy, many smaller schools—especially those in the most isolated rural locations—could not have started without adequate contributions from the immediate African American community. That this local giving happened at levels of effort far outstripping personal capacity is undoubtedly testimony to the desire among black citizens for control of their own educational systems. African American parents understood that public schooling, even at the dismal levels provided for their sons and daughters, was controlled by and for white interests; and they perceived that the wealthiest and most stable black post-secondary institutions were largely beholden to the white philanthropists who sat on their boards of trustees.

The work of Elizabeth Evelyn Wright to establish the school that became Voorhees College in Denmark, SC, provides a stirring example of the achievements that could occur with African American support. While Voorhees College eventually stabilized and grew through the largesse of northern benefactors Ralph and Elizabeth Voorhees, it began as an all-grades industrial school with a solid foundation of local African American contributions. This strong local backing allowed the school to solidify its mission and its commitment to black control from the beginning.

Typifying the aspirations of African Americans struggling for control of their own educational aims and means, Elizabeth ("Lizzie") Wright focused her efforts more on establishing a place to educate rural black students than on undertaking a pedagogy to maximize their learning. This emphasis, with its priority on local community solidarity and control, is consistent with the aims of of many African American teachers of the late nineteenth and early twentieth centuries. Racial uplift, personal pride, Christian beliefs and behavior, and preparation of a black leadership cadre were aims at least as important as occupational training and general education. Additionally, Wright and her fellow educators were well aware of the need to establish a respected corps of African American teachers who could attract students and gain political sway for more equal educational opportunities.[54]

Wright's girlhood experiences and early education readily pointed her in the direction of spiritual dedication and the African American uplift mission. Born in 1872 on the wrong side of the tracks in Talbotton, Georgia, she was the seventh of nineteen children born to a black carpenter and his full-blooded Cherokee wife. Neither her father, John Wesley Wright, nor her mother, Virginia Rolfe Wright, were literate. Wright's early life was spent in a three-room cabin built by her father and situated among the dirt roads and litter-strewn pathways known as Smith Hill, the black section of the county seat of Talbot County in western Georgia. In contrast, the white section of the small town (population approximately 1,000 at the time) was noted for its lovely homes marked by white columns and wrap-around porches.[55]

Wright's mother frequently left home to gather with other nearby Cherokees. According to Wright's brother, Charlie, Virginia Rolfe Wright "looked like a gypsy. She told fortunes and traveled all over to do what she did. It was not uncommon for her to be gone for weeks at a time. Even so, my father loved that woman." Nevertheless, John Wesley Wright eventually built a second cabin next door and took a second wife, Mary West, who helped look after the children when Virginia Wright was away. Elizabeth Wright quickly came under the strong spiritual influence of her highly religious grandmother, Lydia Rolfe.[56]

St. Philip's African Methodist Episcopal Church became the center of Wright's early life. The family joined Sunday services there, and Wright attended a school in the basement where she eagerly learned what she could during the few months each year that schools for black students were open. In the midst of a life defined by church, school, and tending younger siblings, Wright managed to find a flyer or newspaper that described a place that gave her hope for a future: Tuskegee Institute, about 100 miles away in western Alabama, where poor black students could work their way through to obtain an education. The first letter she ever received by mail, in 1888, was addressed to "Miss Lizzie Wright" from Booker T. Washington in response to an inquiry she had sent about the school. With the help of her church school teacher, she countered substantial opposition from her father, found part-time work to earn train fare, and entered Tuskegee in September 1888 as a night student working during the day to pay her expenses.

Opened in a church basement in 1881, and attended by about 350 students by the time Wright entered, Tuskegee followed the plan developed at Hampton Institute where Booker T. Washington had been taught "to love labour, not alone for its financial value, but for labour's own sake and for the independence and self-reliance which the ability to do something, which the world wants done, brings."[57] Wright, although not a top student by academic measures, was an exemplary Tuskegee pupil: An eager African American whose limited education and absent funding left her with no opportunity whatsoever for postsecondary schooling without Booker T. Washington's institution. She was grateful for her chance, impressed by her surroundings, persistent in her studies, and committed to spreading the Tuskegee philosophy to the next generation of rural black students. At Tuskegee she discovered the mentors and role models she never had at home, as well as a network of individuals committed to helping her attain her goals and to furthering the general aims of racial uplift, pride, and leadership sought through African American education.

Recalling her Tuskegee experience just a few months before her terminal illness in 1906, Wright commented, "The sight of the large brick and wooden buildings made a lasting impression on my mind. It was a hard thing for me to understand how a man of my race could have acquired so much.... I was only at Tuskegee a short time before I made up my mind to try and be the same type of woman as Mr. Washington was of a man." She credited Washington's Sunday talks in the chapel for their influence on her determination "to help my fellow men to help themselves, and if a way was not opened for me, I must open it myself."[58]

Like other Tuskegee pupils, Wright was schooled in basic subjects like language, reading, mathematics, and writing. She was also taught personal hygiene, etiquette, nutrition, and thrift. And, importantly, she was schooled in the dignity of labor. Student farm labor was a busy industry at Tuskegee, as were carpentry, printing, brick making, shoe and harness repair, painting, and black-smithing. Wright's assigned tasks largely were in the areas of cleaning, sewing, and dining hall assistance. Tuskegee had perfected a system that embraced student labor as both a means to support the school with sweat equity and a means to teach trades and methods that might contribute to economic independence after graduation.

Long plagued with intestinal problems, Wright was rather frail and unable to do enough work to completely pay her way at Tuskegee. Mrs. Washington, who she revered, convinced a Tuskegee trustee, Judge George W. Kelley of Rockland, MA, to support Wright financially. Kelley's interest in Wright extended to campus visits and to support during her early career

After two years, Wright's frail condition made it impossible for her to continue manual work and school work at Tuskegee. Administrators at Tuskegee arranged for her to take a year off by assisting Tuskegee trustee Mrs. Almira S. Steele with a school she had started seven years before for rural blacks in McNeill's, a sawmill town in southern South Carolina. Wright and Tuskegee student Lulu Davis worked at McNeill's until April 1893, when a group of local whites, long resentful of a Yankee coming to town on behalf of black citizens, set a fire that destroyed Mrs. Steele's school. Wright got her first taste of the depths of hatred that fueled the Ku Klux Klan and the growing numbers of lynchings of her fellow blacks.[59]

When Wright returned to Tuskegee for a final year of school before graduating, she knew she would be a teacher of rural African Americans who were in most need of economic uplift. Her idealism was sparked by the models created by her own teachers at Tuskegee who she viewed as "such gentle and refined ladies and gentlemen." She later observed, "Their lives influenced me for good, and it was my desire to hurry and get out into the world, connect myself with some school and try to set a living example for those who come under my charge." After graduation, Wright decided to return to South Carolina, perhaps the most inhospitable area for black education late in the nineteenth century and perhaps the neediest. Poverty and disease were the common conditions of rural blacks, and the vast majority of the 55 percent of South Carolinians considered literate were whites.[60]

Indicative of the extreme zeal that would mark her choices and efforts, Wright would not consider simply teaching in an existing school for African Americans, although there were some-including some public schools-in the larger towns. Her mission was to build a school where there was none, preferably where blacks were so poor and so isolated that her school provided their first and only opportunity for advancement. She returned to McNeill's, South Carolina, where her personal benefactor, Judge Kelley, purchased some property and some lumber for a building that would replace Elmira Steele's school.

When the lumber to be used for the new schoolhouse succumbed to arson by hostile white neighbors, Wright moved a train stop down the road to the town of Early Branch where an abandoned log cabin could be used for a school. She was determined that her school would be controlled by local black citizens, for blacks, and with the support of blacks. Another Tuskegee graduate soon joined her and often assumed the role of sole teacher while Wright walked the countryside to attend church services and meetings where she spoke and raised whatever pocket change could be donated for the school. The Hampton County Board of Education supported her salary for four months of the year; and Wright added a night school to teach basic literacy and math skills to young men working in the nearby sawmills and farms. Wright had, in 1895, founded the first night school for black adults in the region.[61]

Still, Wright longed for an industrial school on the Tuskegee model—complete with a farm to teach farming and support the dining hall, as well as various industrial shops for instruction and entrepreneurship. Farming, especially, could provide a school with much needed student labor, while teaching practical techniques and discipline. Wright's explanation in a letter to Booker T. Washington noted the appeal of both school labor and education when she explained, "We make farming the leading industry for the young men for this reason: Most of them come from the country and when they return we want them to know more about tilling the soil and to be capable of making better crops. If we had better farming implements, they would do the work better and with more zeal."[62]

Wright's efforts, like those of many others seeking to stabilize underfunded rural institutions, could only succeed with a great deal of on-site student labor. The Washington notion of the learning the dignity of labor and acquiring employable skills was only one motivation for industrial training schools. Institutional survival was another, relying heavily on either the largesse of benefactors who might want to control directions or the ability to match student training to institutional operating costs. Wright undoubtedly viewed sawing, hoeing, milking, building, washing, cooking, and other student endeavors as crucial to the economic health of any school she would develop and essential to maintaining control by African Americans in the nearby community.

After organizing two additional all-grades schools in Hampton County, one in a church and one in a small frame building in the town of Govan, Wright continued to scour nearby areas for favorable conditions for a full-fledged industrial school. The town of Denmark, in neighboring Bamberg County, had no public school for black students and was home to an influential state senator, Stanwix G. Mayfield, who was supportive of education for all citizens. In fact, Denmark seemed such an ideal location that Wright for the first time asked for help from local, and even some distant, whites. Her first school in Denmark was located in a room over a grocery store and managed with the help of another Tuskegee graduate and a nurse and teacher from Ohio. After a year, however, Wright had raised enough money for a down payment on twenty acres of land with three dwellings on it—ample enough space for a schoolhouse, quarters for boarding students and teachers, and a farm. The school opened in 1897 and by 1898, had over 200 pupils.[63]

As the school grew, so did Wright's fund-raising efforts. Like numerous institution builders in the South at the time, she appealed—mostly in direct mail campaigns—to northern benefactors. Olivia Stokes, of the family responsible for the Phelps-Stokes Fund, sent $325 and found a friend who sent $100. Other gifts came from Massachusetts, Pennsylvania, and the Midwest. Others wanted more influence over the school before they would consent to donate. Dr. J.H. Kellogg, for example, promised to pay off the mortgage if the school were deeded to the American Medical Missionary Association and if he could select all personnel. Donations from the local black community continued, even in the face of unfavorable pulpit tirades from Reverend R.D. Rice, pastor of a nearby African American Baptist Church who was infuriated that one of the teachers at the school was a Seventh Day Adventist. Wright's appeals to potential benefactors spoke not only of educational needs, but also of her own personal sacrifices. In a letter to George Foster Peabody, she noted, "The school has not been able to pay me anything for my time. It takes all the money I can raise to pay the other teachers."[64]

The scarce resources for schools like Wright's Denmark Industrial Institute and other activities toward racial uplift inevitably encouraged some skepticism, even jealousy, among competing entities. Particularly telling was the response of Martha Schofield, a noted white educator who had come South to found

Mather Industrial School for blacks at Beaufort, SC, and the Schofield Normal and Industrial School at Aiken, SC. Writing to her friend Emily Howland after meeting Wright, Schofield insisted, "Her situation is a very poor one to make an institution, though Senator Mayfield sends his teams and gives them all their wood from his other places....She is in earnest, has great zeal and thinks she will get all she wants. She did raise the money to meet this year's expenses, but those who give should know all about it.... It astonishes me with what ease the colored people get money. I was in the work for 20 years before anyone entrusted me with $800 for a building. But the 'no salary' touches people." Commenting on Wright's desire to purchase a 200-acre tract for the school, Schofield added that a small all-grades school might be better and that at least some training in trades could be found within less than 100 miles at the African American land grant college, Orangeburg State College, or at the private Claflin College. "What would she do with 200 acres?" she puzzled.[65]

After one northern philanthropist, Ralph Voorhees, finally answered the sixth appeal letter Wright had sent him, Wright's goal of more space and more industries at an expanded school became possible. When she visited Mr. and Mrs. Voorhees in Clinton, NJ, to make her pitch, she ate a meal in the home of white people for the first time in her life. Within a few months, Voorhees sent to Wright $5,000 for purchase of a 280-acre property in Denmark and construction of a large schoolhouse. Wright, who still sought advice from Booker T. Washington in all matters, corresponded to him to explain that Voorhees wanted no particular control over the school, other than it should bear his name. Washington approved the new name, Voorhees Industrial School, which opened its first building in 1902.[66]

With curriculum and bylaws adopted from those of Tuskegee, Wright's primary endeavor at Voorhees became construction of buildings for boys, and girls, dormitories, classrooms, and various trades and industries. The benevolence of Ralph and Elizabeth Voorhees opened the door to additional donors, and a school modeled on Tusgegee quickly became a reality. With additional contributions from northern benefactors and from board of trustees members Emily Howland, Olivia Stokes, Senator Mayfield, the school soon had a chapel, administrative space, classrooms, boys' and girls' dormitories, a blacksmith shop, a large barn, and teachers' housing. By 1903, most of the 252 students were elementary and middle school age and were placed in the "training department." They learned basic life skills, reading, writing, and math. All, however, took some part in manual labor—cooking, cleaning, sewing, farming, fencing, leather working, and other necessary endeavors. The curriculum never veered far from Wright's unwavering notion that "most people in the South live by tilling the soil, if they have a knowledge of agriculture they will soon become independent.... Each year we put more stress on farming."[67]

Tuskegee graduate Martin A. Menafee had joined the industrial school staff in 1900 to become business manager and treasurer. Undoubtedly, he was selected by Booker T. Washington as someone who could oversee finances, student registration, farm product sales, and general administration. Although Wright's chronic gastritis and general poor health might seem to warn against the union, she married her colleague Menafee in June 1906. By September, she was hopitalized in Augusta, GA. From there, she went to Battle Creek Sanitarium in Michigan. Although she rallied briefly following intestinal surgery, she relapsed and died in December 1906. Ralph Voorhees died only a few months later. Voorhees Industrial School, however, thrived. By 1929, it became the first junior college for African Americans in the Southeast to be accredited by the Southern Association of Colleges and Schools. Today, it is a respected private four-year college.

In an article upon Wright's death, the *Bamberg (SC) Herald* indicated the general community estimation of her:

> Lizzie Menafee was a good woman. In all her business transactions we found her one of the most prompt and reliable persons we had ever dealt with.... Her sound common sense and fine business judgment en-

> abled her to make a success of the school at Denmark where ninety out of a hundred would have failed.... She started with nothing, yet in ten years she has built up a school whose equipment is worth about $50,000. Although a woman, we regarded her as a great leader of the race.[68]

Soul and Serendipity

The "vocationalists" of this study appear to have a great deal in common, most notably their passion for a cause that was as much about general uplift of their race as about educational reform. Their sheer determination to contribute to opportunities for African Americans was far more keenly motivating than their sense of *what* to contribute.

Each of these women arrived at the idea of vocational education as a key element in uplift from a different direction. Nannie Helen Burroughs experienced a solid liberal education in a fine high school, but could not readily find a job. Undoubtedly, she perceived economic advantage for women of her race who might be taught a vocation along with their academic studies. Mary McLeod Bethune was educated in missionary schools and trained in missionary work. Teaching soon became her mission, always with an emphasis toward practical skills (including homemaking), racial and gender uplift for women, and spiritual goodness. Elizabeth Voorhees knew that Tuskegee and its industrial fare was a wonderful relief from the dirt poor and hungry existence of her childhood, and she was committed to spreading that relief to others. For these three women, and many others in similar situations, educational reform was whatever could be fashioned in a given time and place that might address immediate needs in the immediate future.

Although the vocationalists of the South during the Progressive Era may have brought more soul than savvy to their work, they made up in will what they might have lacked in political acumen. They did not wait for adequate capital to start. They did not strategize their next moves. They simply started and continued. Those whose institutions survived may have been more determined than others, or perhaps simply more fortunate.

Even though we might want to refer to women who started educational institutions as "pioneers," these women did have some examples among those who came before them and became their mentors. Mary McLeod Bethune credited Lucy Craft Laney, founder of Haines Institute, as her role model. Nannie Helen Burroughs could look up to Anna Julia Cooper as she worked her way through M Street High School, and Elizabeth Evelyn Wright took Booker T. Washington as a mentor and Mrs. Washington as a role model. Although their networking was not generally calculated, each woman eagerly learned from the strengths of their associates and enjoyed a wide range of contacts who could support their work.

Many, many small industrial schools were founded in the South during the Progressive Era. Few survived beyond a dozen years. Many, like Elizabeth Evelyn Wright's first endeavors in South Carolina, never got beyond the log cabin or church basement phase. Did something about the women founders themselves make the difference in institutional survival? Or was good fortune at play? Although the answer is elusive, it is quite evident that the three women examined in this chapter shared some important characteristics—clear and compelling goals for fairly immediate success, pragmatic views toward method and process, commitment to personal sacrifice, and extensive spiritual underpinnings. Importantly, and especially in the case of Bethune and Wright, their successes also were dependent on outward personalities and appearances that could be seen as nonthreatening by men, whites, and even other African Americans.

ILLUSTRATIONS

Charlotte Hawkins Brown
Courtesy North Carolina Division of Archives and History

Martha Berry with students at the Berry School
Courtesy of Berry College

Alice Lloyd

Courtesy Special Collections Library, Alice Lloyd College

Alice Lloyd College in its early days
Courtesy Special Collections Library, Alice Lloyd College

Original building at the Berry School
Courtesy of Berry College

Mary McLeod Bethune
Courtesy Library of Congress, Carl Van Vechten Photographs

Nannie Helen Burroughs
Courtesy Library of Congress

Elizabeth Evelyn Wright

Courtesy Voorhees College, Media Relations and Marketing Department

Annie Webb Blanton
Courtesy Prints and Photographs Collection,
Center for American History, University of Texas at Austin

Cora Wilson Stewart
Special Collections and Archives, University of Kentucky Libraries

Wil Lou Gray
Courtesy Museum of Education, University of South Carolina

CHAPTER FIVE

Systems Thinkers: Networking for Lasting Change

During the Progressive Era, the idea of a woman in a power position such as public education policymaker, school superintendent, or county school supervisor clearly seemed inappropriate and unappealing among lingering Victorian Era ideals. The women who did venture into the public sphere to teach generally found men at the pinnacle of state and school administrations imposing their perspectives and their practices upon the female teachers at the base. Within this highly gendered hierarchy, classroom teachers played a limited role in the actual development and operation of "the system." Male school administrators, according to Rousmaniere, "laid out a highly systemic blueprint of teachers' daily job expectations and a bureaucratic system of supervision and evaluation."[1] In addition to gendered prejudices, personnel selection and practices in the schools were implicitly biased against teachers from certain cultural, ethnic, and class backgrounds.[2]

Despite these drawbacks, the southern women educators defined as "systems thinkers" in this chapter enthusiastically entered the political fray and worked—if not always effectively, at least diligently—to influence policies and widespread practices in systems where power existed in a top down formation. These women are not mainstreamed into the written histories of Progressive Era school reform; yet recorded accounts of their efforts exist and serve to expand the literature of this era.

These systems thinkers worked beyond single institutions to affect education policies and multiple institutions in a society where important tenets in people's lives were racism, sexism, elitism, ageism, and professionalism. They began locally by vigorously canvassing their immediate towns and counties and later graduated to larger statewide scales to gain national reputations in the areas of policy change and construction for lasting educational improvement. The accomplishments of these southern women are significant because they took place at a time when many assumed that women were capable neither of leadership nor rational thought. Although in many ways they accepted the patriarchal dominance of the systems in which they struggled, the women depicted here often challenged the status quo, thereby risking rejection or worse, appearing unwomanly.

By focusing on the work of three such women, Kentucky's Cora Wilson Stewart, South Carolina's Wil Lou Gray, and Texas' Annie Webb Blanton, this chapter will address two questions: In what ways did these women affect education systems and/or policies in Progressive Era paternalistic and racist education bureaucracies? To what extent did these women's activities provide viable ways for working-class women, people of color, and others to use education to renegotiate the boundaries of power relationships based on race, gender and social class? Clearly, although they perceived governmental bureaucracies and public policies as crucial to school reform, these well-intentioned women could not understand contemporary, postmodern notions of power as a complex, relational, and dynamic phenomenon within elite patriarchal structures. Yet, as they struggled for change (and sometimes for control), these women operated effectively within the confines of large bureaucratic systems to build coalitions among diverse groups in order to reform various aspects of education in the South. Although they did not consciously attempt to redraw the fixed boundaries of the patriarchal status quo, their efforts within established channels did push the boundaries enough to shape new educational programs and policies.

Typical of Progressive Era thought, systems thinkers demonstrated a commitment to improving society through education. Although visionaries who recognized the Progressive Era reforming spirit of progress, these women managed to create a sympathetic environment for their goals and ideas among more traditional men and women. For example, their personal styles generally projected the affirmed image of early twentieth century school teachers. They were properly dressed and coifed; they demonstrated a strong sense of responsibility; and they had a no-nonsense manner about themselves. Their properly feminine portrayals and performances were neither offensive to men nor challenging to the gender hierarchy.

White, middle class, and armed with college degrees, they rose to public service through the traditional female outlets of teaching and participating in women's clubs. Surrounding themselves with women who shared their ideas about women's roles in education, they united and inspired volunteers to educate adults, participate in professional organizations, and raise the status of the teaching profession. They drew their strength and motivation from the women who, like themselves, were committed to improving society through education. Although they understood the political practices of mobilizing and organizing as necessary for people to transform their worlds, they employed a nonthreatening approach to working for women's causes. This gave the impression of women who sought to improve "the system," but not overthrow it.

The systems thinkers we describe deliberately embraced human experience as a starting point for reform and favored concrete over theoretical solutions to problems such as educating adult illiterates and raising the level of professionalism in the highly feminized teaching vocation. Their aspirations are not characterized by their reflection or conjecture about their own experiences and problems as women *per se*, but by the pragmatic turn they took toward focusing on the experiences and pressing problems of the everyday lives of students, teachers, and school administrators.

Although at the turn of the twentieth century, they faced Victorian Era gender norms with uncommon courage and strength, often shattering glass ceilings in educational reform, there is little evidence that these southern women educators influenced the course of feminist theory—and even progressivism, for that matter. This chapter examines that anomaly and challenges its accuracy.

Systems thinkers viewed educational reform as policy initiative and could not help getting caught in the complex political power plays that dominated public sentiment. Cora Wilson Stewart of Kentucky, for example, upon shocking the nation with the data that one out of four men who registered for the military draft in 1917 could neither read nor write, convinced President Herbert Hoover to establish the National Advisory Committee on Illiteracy.[3] As educators, the systems thinkers likely asked themselves, "How can we focus on the immediate living conditions and needs of our people?" or "How do we balance the interests of big business and the employment of our people?" For instance, although they admired a classical liberal education for those that could afford it, Cora Wilson Stewart and Wil Lou Gray insisted that job training and domestic skills be part of the curriculum for children in the mountains of Kentucky and the textile mills of South Carolina.

This chapter describes the life work of three exceptional southern women who displayed leadership and participated in the political crusades of the day. These women attained success locally and on state and national levels without alienating male supporters. Because they were pro-woman without being anti-man, they were able to find a comfort level in the working world of men. From this perspective, they may be viewed as moderate feminists. Although they did not draw new boundary lines, they did push some boundaries to create new courses of action.

Whether working alone or in coalition with other organizations, these women learned and practiced effective organizational and persuasive techniques.

The chapter begins with Cora Wilson Stewart, whose first educational reform efforts at the local level in her native Kentucky transported her into the national and international arenas of policy change and educational reform in adult literacy. The study next moves to the national reputation in adult education of Wil Lou Gray who served as the State Supervisor of Adult Education in the South Carolina State Department of Education for twenty-eight years and founded Opportunity Schools in that state to reduce adult illiteracy. Finally, the reform efforts of Annie Webb Blanton are traced as she participated in the complex political and social movements of the Progressive Era as Texas' State Superintendent of Public Instruction, founder of Delta Kappa Gamma, and a long time professor at the University of Texas.

Cora Wilson Stewart and the Moonlight Schools

Cora Wilson Stewart (1875–1958) is best known for her work in Rowan County, Kentucky and for founding the Moonlight Schools after recognizing the problems and the potential of the illiterate adult mountain folk in the region.[4] Growing up in the mountains of Eastern Kentucky, Cora Wilson enjoyed a privileged childhood compared with most residents of Rowan County. Her parents were both educated and determined to provide their children with proper schooling. Jeremiah Wilson, her father, was a country doctor; and her mother, Anne Halley Wilson, worked outside the home as a teacher.[5] Although Cora was born the third of the couples' twelve children, the early death of her two older siblings destined her to assume the leadership role of the oldest child in the Wilson family.[6] She reflected on her privileged upbringing:

> We had pictures on our walls while other children had none. We had stories. We had books. The difference between our lives and most of the other children in the community was that our parents were educated.[7]

The family relocated to Morehead, Kentucky, to benefit her father's medical practice and to enroll Cora in the Morehead Normal School for college preparatory training and a teacher's course.[8] After completing the normal school courses by age 16, she was encouraged by both of her parents to continue her education. Between sessions of her teaching position in the Morehead public schools, she attended the National Normal University in Lebanon, Ohio, from 1892–1895.[9]

Jeremiah Wilson, a leading citizen of the Morehead community, encouraged his daughter to try medicine or a legal profession, but Cora was more interested in music, the theater, and writing. She attended Wilbur R. Smith Business College in Lexington, Kentucky, and graduated in 1899. Ironically, it was her father's refusal to comply with conventional Victorian Era gender norms that benefited his daughter's career the most. After teaching for ten years, the civic-minded Stewart was selected as the Democratic candidate for Rowan County school superintendent in 1901.

Her brother, Bunyan Spratt Wilson, a successful attorney in addition to being mayor of Morehead and a member of the board of Education, was in a good position to help his sister win the election. With his support, she won the election to become the first woman school superintendent in a radius of 26 counties. Her election paved the way for other female superintendents in neighboring counties. As superintendent of Rowan County Schools, Stewart's reputation as public speaker and proponent of vocational education grew. Although she preferred a classic liberal arts education, she was pragmatic in her approach to the education of the mountain children, insisting the mountain youth needed skills to get jobs in the growing economy.

Stewart likely found herself torn between her career ambitions in the field of education and the conventional life of wife and mother. The prevailing Victorian Era view held that a woman was essentially different from a man—mentally and physically. For the most part, the future meant marriage and retirement to her home to nurture a family. Her role in society was determined by the prestige and position her husband attained, and her personal reputation was determined by her success as a wife and mother. This ideology was reiterated by Stewart's mother, a very religious woman who doubtless expected her daughter to adhere to society's view of a domestic mold for females. Anne Halley Wilson's diary reflected these traditional values and roles:

> A Woman's affections are sacred. They are her life and he who takes upon himself their guardianship assumes a holy and responsible duty. A true woman loves independent of all worldly circumstances. . . A true woman loves when she loves truly and tenderly and if she unites with the opposite sex in the bond of holy matrimony and feels assured that her love is appreciated she is ready to lay her life at the feet of the man she loves and if the task could be allotted to her of making the path in which he were to walk it would be straight and sweet and soft as a bed of roses. . . Yes, the love of a true woman for her husband is more precious to her than the miser's affection for his hoarded gold. These are my imperfectly expressed ideas of a women's true love.[10]

Stewart's personal life never reached the pinnacle of marital bliss described by her mother. Cora Wilson and A.T. Stewart married for the first time in 1903, divorced in 1904, and remarried just three months after the divorce. A pattern of domestic abuse elevated by alcoholism led to their second divorce in 1910. According to sworn court depositions, at midnight on March 21, 1910, A.T. Stewart came home in a drunken state and tried to kick in the door of the room where Cora and her two sisters were sleeping. When Cora opened the door he violently cursed her and yelled, "I've come to blow you up."[11]

To make matters worse, her only child died in 1908, causing local gossip about unfit motherhood.[12] A few neighbors went so far as to claim that if she had taken better care of her baby instead of making so many public appearances, the child would not have died. During a time when domestic problems were rarely publicized and highly stigmatizing, this extraordinary woman found the strength to carry on her professional life with uncommon courage.

By 1910, Stewart had developed a large network of supporters and established some useful contacts. Many of her boosters were women who believed it was time for a female to lead the Kentucky Educational Association K.E.A. M. O. Winfrey, the superintendent of Middlesborough School, wrote the following to Stewart:

> I am glad that you have awakened to the fact that there is a crying need for a WOMAN at the head of the K.E.A. who is EQUAL TO THE OCCASION and WHO CAN PRESIDE. You are that woman.[13]

Elected the first woman president of the K.E.A. in 1911, Stewart was fast becoming a powerful public figure. From the Bluegrass State, she went on to become a national and international figure. Five times she chaired the Illiteracy Section of the World Conference of Education Associations. She conducted dozens of illiteracy conferences throughout the United States, served on the powerful Executive Board of the National Education Association, and founded the National Illiteracy Crusade in 1926.[14]

However, it was the Moonlight Schools that brought Cora Wilson Stewart national attention. According to Willie Nelms:

> The name is symbolic of the woman who started them. The term sounds romantic, and the schools reflected characteristics that their founder admired. They were heroic, they were practical, they were idealistic, and most of all, they were a great popular success.[15]

As various school improvement associations came under control of state bureaucratic agencies, women turned in earnest to anti-illiteracy campaigns, the first of which occurred in Kentucky at the instigation of Stewart.[16] As superintendent of schools for Rowan County from 1901–1904, Stewart conceptualized "Moonlight

Schools" to help less fortunate citizens of Rowan County gain basic literacy skills or, in her words, "emancipate from illiteracy all those enslaved in its bondage"[17]

Since there were no public funds in place for such a program, Stewart sought volunteers to teach in the public schools during the evening hours. She appealed to the self-interest of teachers telling them that teaching the parents would encourage interest in the public schools.[18] Organizing a teachers' club that included almost every teacher in the county, she won their agreement to keep their schools open on "moonlit nights" for a special six-week session.[19] The first Moonlight Schools opened on September 5, 1911, initially seeking to reach about 300 Rowan County residents.[20] The idea received an unexpectedly enthusiastic response when more than 1,300 persons, ages 18 to 36, enrolled. One observer noted, "Whole families turned out: children during the day, parents and older children at night. Not only men and women of mature years, but the aged have shown a yearning for this opportunity to learn."[21] Stewart wrote,

> The youngest student was aged eighteen, the oldest eighty-six. It was a scene to bring tears to the eyes, but surely one to make the heart rejoice, to see those hoary-headed old people and those robust young people seated at their desks studying together, or standing in a row in class to spell, or lined up at the blackboard to solve problems or to write.[22]

Information about the Moonlight Schools spread outside the borders of Kentucky when Stewart addressed the Southern Education Association in Houston, Texas, on December 1, 1911.[23] During early 1912, Stewart spoke to the state educational associations of Alabama, Arkansas, Virginia, and South Carolina.[24]

By 1913, in an attempt to wipe out illiteracy in the county, the evening schools enrolled 2,500 people.[25] Stewart argued that the public school did not have a right to say to men and women, "if you embrace me not before a certain age or before a certain hour in the day I will close my door to you forever."[26] Influential educational journals of the time, such as *Normal Instructor* and *The*

Progressive Teacher, published articles claiming Moonlight Schools as the standard.[27] "It was tried in tobacco districts," wrote Stewart; "it was tried in the mining camps, and miners embraced the opportunity with eagerness."[28] From isolated farming sections, rural Kentuckians traveled for miles to attend class and could hardly be persuaded to go home when the hour for dismissal arrived; and in the mountains, people crowded to the schools in mass.[29]

By 1913, twenty-five counties in Kentucky had started the schools; and by 1915, nineteen states had adopted Stewart's model for anti-illiteracy campaigns.[30] When Kentucky established the first state illiteracy commission in 1914, others followed suit, making these efforts a permanent part of the school apparatus.[31] In a bulletin which was headed "Kentucky Wars on Illiteracy," the U.S. Commissioner of Education wrote:

> It will be a part of the lasting glory of the State of Kentucky that it has taken the lead in this movement. It is the first state to offer to all the people, of whatever age, an opportunity to learn to read and write, and thus break away from the prison wall of sense and silence within which the illiterate man and woman must live.[32]

Stewart's pedagogical methods involved interaction with her students' home and work environments, and she embraced the experiences of the mountain people as a starting point for teaching them to read and write. She also worked to persuade women to feel a sense of responsibility for teaching illiterates just as she worked to change attitudes toward adult illiteracy. In the spring of 1917, she called for teacher volunteers in the press. "An unusual situation confronts those engaged in teaching in this State. It is one which will put to the test your patriotism and your devotion to education."[33] She further argued that if the men who were "sent across the water to fight your battles and mine" were illiterate, they might not be able to take comfort in writing home or reading the Bible. Therefore, she reasoned, it was the patriotic duty of teachers to enable these defenders of freedom to read and write.

Her campaign employed the crusade model of organizing, and much of the success of her program depended on exhorting teachers and school officials to undertake the work of "campaigning with zeal." Stewart wrote:

> Some of those who had learned were not only walking evangelists preaching the gospel of "No illiteracy in the county," but became itinerant teachers going from district to district giving lessons.[34]

Further, since no half-hearted methods would do, they must enter the crusade with "whole hearts."[35] The appeal of the campaign would rest on a "plea none can resist": a "missionary spirit" that would free illiterates from ignorance and "bring to them long-armed usefulness and power."[36] Once teachers realized this need, Stewart predicted, their hearts would be "overflowing."[37]

Along with the rhetoric of evangelism, Stewart urged hard-nosed grassroots organizing. Crusaders should enroll in writing all who were willing to come. Enrollees should be pressed to attend regularly, and petitioners should point out to potential students the names on Stewart's list of those who would have an influence on others. The half-educated should be on those lists along with the total illiterates, and the most intelligent and influential persons should be granted leadership roles.

The scheduling of the classes, she warned, was crucial; and the "finest moonlight night in the month" should be chosen, as dark and rainy nights discouraged attendance.[38] The schools themselves should be as attractive as possible with well lit classrooms. Sessions should be limited to two hours and enhanced with a short opening talk, a "stirring song," at least one rapid drill, and simple lessons in history and geography. All students should have one lesson to complete; it would be enough to make them hungry for more. Similar in broad philosophy to the Deweyan notion of progressive education, Stewart's concepts for reform located the students at the center of the effort.

Stewart's unique focus on the education of adult illiterates proved to be a popular call. She appealed to the progressive reform spirit of the day and gave voice to a marginalized group of people who were unable to articulate their frustration at now having basic literacy skills. Stewart's attack on illiteracy as a type of social evil was similar to that of other progressive reformers of the period, and she viewed social problems as ills that needed to be reckoned with. Her grassroots efforts at starting networks that spread rapidly fit her positioning of humanistic experiences and conditions as the central locus of her reform efforts.

Stewart's activities and recommendations in adult education provided a viable way for working-class white men and women of all ages to begin to renegotiate the boundaries of power. She discovered that the way to break the grip of traditional governance on public opinion was to adopt the crusade model of popular mobilization. By using modern forms of media, she successfully dramatized the obvious deficiencies in the post-Reconstruction school system. Fanning popular outrage through a careful manipulation of newspapers and other organs of opinion, she also successfully employed the vehicle of revival style mobilization. As a result, her single, centralized crusade in Kentucky developed into a decentralized campaign and she adjusted her timing and style to local opinion and acknowledged the fact that state and local conditions were individual and different.

Yet, Stewart's work in the field of adult literacy is only marginally mentioned, if it is mentioned at all, in educational history books. Her invisibility most likely stems from a combination of the following reasons: (1) she focused her efforts in rural Kentucky on groups of working class mountain folk who were both marginalized and undervalued in American society; (2) she was a woman who dared to enter the public sphere of men; and (3) she lacked the graduate degree credentials of some of her contemporaries. However, Stewart's concept of Moonlight Schools solidified her career as an authority on adult literacy that spanned for more than 20 years. Supported by club women and other voluntary associations, she became an educational entrepreneur as she canvassed the country supporting herself through an inheritance of family money, speeches, book royalties, and magazine articles.[39]

As a systems thinker, Stewart understood the institutionalized prejudices surrounding the education of adults. Her campaign was aimed at building awareness among politicians and the general public, but especially among teachers and college professors—"educating the educated"—who needed to understand the problems associated with illiteracy. "The greatest trouble with some educators is that they are opposed to education."[40] She also struggled with convincing some illiterates themselves.

> Not everyone came rushing out to school in every district when the schools first opened. An institution so new as a school where illiterate adults could learn to read and write may easily be misunderstood, criticized and even resented by those who need it most.[41]

Skilled in community involvement, she presented statistics of illiteracy from the states and the nation designed to arouse both civic and individual responsibility, and urged community groups to contribute funds, donate their services, as well as give moral support to her cause. Often frustrated, she noted:

> The right of adult illiterates to learn had been challenged, their ability to do so had been questioned, the advisability of having teachers assume the extra duty of teaching them had been doubted, the statistics, when analyzed and brought close to home had been disputed and resented; demagogues had assumed that any reference to the illiteracy of the state or the community meant to traduce it, professional politicians had gloried in holding the purse-strings of the public treasury as tight as possible against any invasion for such a cause.[42]

Stewart did not hold a master's or a doctoral degree; and many of the male influential leaders of the adult education movement who held either a Ph.D. or Ed.D. degrees from universities of the Northeast challenged her adult literacy techniques.[43] The dominant ideology among scholars of the day held that the best way to prevent adult illiteracy was to teach children how to read and write (not their parents) leading one Georgia professor to call Stewart's approach of first educating parents to prevent illiteracy in children "unsound."[44] Stewart's debate with the educational establishment intensified as she continued to challenge the conventional wisdom that claimed older people could not learn once the "golden age of memory" has passed.[45]

At a time when sacrifice was expected of women, Stewart thought female volunteers from women's clubs and other civic groups should donate their time, along with schoolteachers, to instruct adult illiterates. In her book, *Moonlight Schools for the Emancipation of Adult Illiterates,* she quoted William Jennings Bryan who addressed the teachers of the Moonlight Schools at a convention in Raleigh, North Carolina. "If there are any who have ever realized these words of the Master, it is more blessed to give than to receive, it must be the teachers of the moonlight schools."[46]

A perception of governmental authority and public policies as crucial to school reform fueled Stewart's struggle for change within the confines of growing bureaucratic systems. Her efforts within established channels shaped new educational programs and policies in the area of adult literacy making her the most widely known authority on adult literacy in the world during the first third of the twentieth century.[47] Beyond her Kentucky crusade, Stewart's personal life required her to examine the existing patriarchal systems which blocked many women from moving out of the comfort zone of the domestic sphere.

By choosing adult education as her life's mission, she braved the rising tide of bureaucratization in the field of education and brought a humanistic qualitative approach to needy adults at a time when many of her contemporaries in the North—such as Jane Addams, Carrie Chatman Catt, and Ida Tarbell—were interested in analyzing educational problems through more reductionist lenses. Stewart also differed from northern female Progressive Era reformers in other ways. At the heart of her work were the mountain people of her time, unlike the urban reformers of the day. She was accepted by the mountaineers because she both respected their civilization and considered it dignified. She also was accepted in more elite society because of her advanced education and her privileged background in comparison to most Rowan County residents. Thus, she was able to bridge the gap between the educated and the uneducated.

Her ability to move freely between both worlds enabled Stewart to become a powerful educational figure. She romanticized the lifestyles and potential of her mountain neighbors at a time when outsiders disparaged them. Stewart ardently defended Kentucky's mountain population claiming they were neither "inferior people" nor "degenerate stock," but in fact "descended from the best ancestry—Virginia and North Carolina—that traces back to England, Scotland, Ireland and Wales" and therefore worthy of an education regardless of their age.[48] Further, she argued that in the mountains of the southern states of America there is a "reservoir of strength and patriotism in the millions of pure Anglo-Saxon Americans."[49] Perhaps to justify the need for night schools for these "pure" white Americans, Stewart unveiled her own racial prejudices when she maintained that not only were the mountain people eager to "take their part in the world of work," but also they were also superior to the "racial groups" who did not seek to "advance the welfare of the nation which has received them into its bosom." [50] She communicated these ideas in a way that eastern Kentuckians understood—the oratory of the religious revivalists. Later, she originated a series of texts called *Country Life Readers,* which taught middle-class, moralistic values such as lessons of virtue, cleanliness, frugality, and civic responsibility—themes that were both popular and expected for textbook writers of the day.[51]

Stewart's movement, stimulated by the Kentucky Illiteracy Commission, spread rapidly before and after World War I to other southern states similarly afflicted with illiteracy. For example, Wil Lou Gray's Opportunity Schools and later, during the early years of the Great Depression, Myles Horton's Highlander Folk School, grew out of Stewart's idea to use adult education as one of the main mechanisms for changing society. These progressive reformers pushed restrictive boundaries in the South and encouraged disenfranchized groups of people to dare to think, dream, stand up for their rights, be creative, and not conform.

Wil Lou Gray and the Struggle for Publicly Supported Adult Education

Wil Lou Gray (1883–1984) was a native of South Carolina, a state better known for its involvement in the start of the American Revolutionary and Civil Wars than for its attention to public and adult literacy education. Agricultural, rural, and relatively small in population, the Palmetto State nevertheless provided the context for the accomplishments of one of the most remarkable women working in southern education. Although agriculture still dominated the southern economy and society well into the twentieth century, manufacturing began to play an increasing role after 1880.[52]

With the rise of the textile industry, cotton mills and mill villages became a major feature of the South Carolina landscape. A class of dependent, propertyless, white mill workers—including women and children—streamed into the mill villages from the rural areas, and Progressive Era reformers sought to use the state apparatus, especially public schools, to break the "cycle of ignorance" among mill workers.[53] Wil Lou Gray responded by developing a system of night schools in both rural and mill areas of Laurens County, patterned after the work of Cora Wilson Stewart in Kentucky.[54]

A large part of Gray's agenda as a public educator was as an acculturating agent of the fast growing modern industrial society, especially in the realm of citizenship. Education in the three R's was designed to gain mill workers and other poor whites access to middle class benefits. Gray's classroom materials and assignments not only preached thrift and good health habits but also taught more political subjects such as civil government, voter responsibilities, and, especially, public education.[55]

Gray's zeal for providing her students with moral inspiration and civic uplift stemmed from her evangelical Protestant and social gospel roots. She enjoyed a privileged, small town South Carolina upbringing.[56] For example, she recalled Governor Tillman and other state leaders coming to dine at her parent's house in Laurens, South Carolina. Her family affluence both shielded her from the poverty most blacks and many whites experienced and enabled her to benefit from the few educational opportunities available to women in the early twentieth century.[57] Since teaching was a genteel way for cultivated young women to simultaneously conform within the gender hierarchy and enter the public sphere, Wil Lou Gray—not one to challenge the status quo—intended to teach. At age 20, she graduated from South Carolina's female Methodist institution, Columbia College.

In order to teach, Gray realized she needed skills in classroom methods and curriculum, and she planned to attend South Carolina's State Normal School for Women (which later became Winthrop College). When she confronted her father, a prominent businessman, William Lafayette Gray told his daughter, "There is no need for you to teach. I can take care of you."[58] Gray recalled this conversation in a 1974 interview:

> Winthrop College this I graduated from college and it was a liberal arts college and when I got home I said to my father, "I want to go to summer." He said, "Why do you want to do that?" I replied, "Well, I. . ." He said, "Don't you think Columbia College is as good as Winthrop?" I said, "Yes sir. But it was two purposes. Winthrop was slanted to teaching and education and how to do it, and Columbia College was slanted toward more of the cultural, academic, emphasizing the academic and learnings than the other. I don't know how to teach." Then I reminded my father that he graduated at Wofford College; but although he graduated Wofford, he had to go somewhere to learn to practice law; and he immediately saw why I wanted to go to Winthrop. I did go to Winthrop and I never had a more rewarding experience in my life than I had that summer over there [at Winthrop].[59]

Gray attended Winthrop College for several successive summers and during the academic year taught in the rural schools of neighboring Greenwood County in the northern region of South Carolina. The young teacher was shocked to find herself in 1903 in a one-room schoolhouse where planks were painted to serve as blackboards. Years later, Gray recalled that first teaching experience:

> I taught in that school the first year and I had some very interesting experiences that first year. . . .We had pupils from the first grade to high school. . . . When I first went there, I went into the school house. There was no furniture—the benches were handmade. There was a pot-bellied stove in the middle of the room. The hogs in the community had used the cellar under the school as a place to get cooled in the summer. So, it was a pretty bleak experience my first few days.[60]

The five-month school year and the fact that the children she taught had no books or magazines in their homes was not lost on Gray who later recalled, "People were so poor at that time. . . . You young people in this age now have no idea how poor the people were."[61]

In 1905, at the age of 22, she enrolled in Vanderbilt University's graduate school to prepare for college teaching. In a course, "The Fatherhood of God; The Brotherhood of Man," which was geared toward raising social awareness and working toward social justice, Professor Jones asked Gray what she was going to do for her community when she left Vanderbilt. She replied, "We don't have any poor in Laurens."[62] In retrospect, Gray confessed, "Children were working in mills for twelve dollars at 55 hours per week. . . . I could hear the mill whistle every morning but it didn't concern me until after Vanderbilt."[63] Gray taught a version of that course as a college instructor, and her later efforts to eradicate adult illiteracy—which comprised her most important life's work—were also inspired by its objectives.

After returning to South Carolina in 1906, she taught for one more year in Greenwood County and then joined the English faculty at Martha Washington College, a women's college in Virginia.[64] In 1910, Gray went to New York City to study political science at Columbia University, receiving her master's degree in 1911.[65] There she was influenced by several liberal scholars including James Harvey Robinson, Charles Beard, Frederick Jackson Turner, and Carl Becker, who approached history as a continuous human process—past and present—and believed that knowledge should be made accessible to ordinary men and women.[66]

Gray abandoned her plan to pursue a college teaching career and accepted the position of Supervisor of Rural Schools in Laurens County from 1914 to 1916.[67]

She returned to Columbia University for further study and served for one year as Supervisor of Rural Schools in Montgomery County, Maryland. In the meantime, at the request of the South Carolina Federation of Women's Clubs, Governor Richard I. Manning appointed the Illiteracy Commission.[68] Gray returned to South Carolina in 1918 to accept the newly created position of field secretary for the South Carolina Illiteracy Commission.[69] She later recalled,

> We knew that South Carolina needed a great deal of work in that field, but somehow we couldn't convince the people. But the war came along . . . World War I; and when they examined our veterans, so many of them were illiterate. And the New York Times carried the headlines, *South Carolina Leads the Union in Illiteracy*.[70]

The origins of her interest in adult illiteracy stemmed from her work as a rural school teacher. Within that community, she witnessed the high level of illiteracy among the parents of her students and among members of the local community.[71] Gray credits the faculty of Columbia University with teaching her the pedagogical practices she would later need to help illiterate adults learn to read.[72]

The white middle-class women's clubs constituted a key part of Gray's lifelong network of supporters and lobbyists who proved an important source of coalition building and had an undying faith in her work.[73] In 1916 the South Carolina General Assembly made its first statewide appropriation for night schools, and the State Federation of Women's Clubs prevailed upon Governor Manning to appoint an Illiteracy Commission.[74] By 1919 the Illiteracy Commission had prodded the General Assembly into establishing the nation's first statewide, state-supported adult education program, headed by the commission's first director, Wil Lou Gray.[75]

While Gray's adult education work was by no means limited to mills, well over one-third of all night schools operating in South Carolina in 1920 were in mill villages, where illiteracy was concentrated and where facilities and financial support were available from the corporations.[76] A larger purpose of the mill schools, and especially of mill executives, was to inculcate the middle-class Progressive Era view of society with its curious blend of democracy and paternalism. One mill president noted:

> Coming in contact with such characters as the teachers is elevating and will help to make the people less suspicious, as these people usually are.. . . this work will make the people appreciate their work, and make them more efficient to their employers.[77]

Although she used lessons of good citizenship in teaching adult illiterates, Gray's goals stemmed from her desire to enable people of low income to have the "experience of a campus life," "to lead a more meaningful life," and "to earn more than a meager existence."[78] Gray found that the first obstacle was convincing people of the necessity of adult education. Many felt that people either could not learn or did not have the desire to learn how to read and write once they reached a certain age. Gray viewed this challenge as changing the ideology and philosophy of the people who didn't want to learn, or worse, believed "they couldn't learn, or they were too old to learn."[79]

The first "opportunity school" initiated by Gray opened in 1921 as a month-long vacation boarding school held in the Blue Ridge Mountain community of Tamassee in Oconee County, located in the extreme northwestern corner of the state.[80] Named after Emily Griffith's opportunity school in Denver, Colorado, and inspired in part by the Danish "folk school" concept, the Opportunity School was designed to provide adults with limited or no formal schooling a summer residential educational experience.[81] The concept of an adult residential institution originated in the middle of the nineteenth century in Denmark. Danish "folk schools" were to assist all adults in solving life's problems—including the moral, social, and personal needs of the students.

Based on the premise that a central place was needed where students could live together for the purpose of learning—free from the effects of grades, academic standing, credits, honors, degrees, and exams—residential adult education meant living together, taking meals together, and sharing responsibilities and experiences. These activities were deemed just as important as class lectures and discussions, reading assignments, and other subject-centered activities. The curricular and residential patterns established at Tamassee, for example, were based on a vacation school for working-class white girls. The wellness of both body and mind was integral to Gray's program and within her diverse curriculum women studied language arts, science, mathematics and arts and crafts as well as health habits, good manners, and domestic science.

Gray recalled the first year of the school was founded mostly on hope, donations amounting to $40, and her brother's gift of a barrel of flour. Groceries and other household items were accepted in lieu of the $1 tuition.[82] Held in a small building situated on a retreat center owned by the Daughters of the American Revolution, the first opportunity school session was restricted to white females.[83] Inaccessibly situated in remote hill country, Tamassee served Gray's original intent to reach young white women under fifth-grade level who had left school early. The first young women to attend her program were primarily from cotton mill villages and tenant farms.

> Tamassee's day began at six-thirty with breakfast at eight. From nine to twelve regular classes were held. At twelve dinner was begun and served at two. Industrial work and studies in hygiene and citizenship filled the early afternoon, late afternoon being left for recreation. In four rotating groups the pupils did the entire household work, even the washing. By such systematizing each girl received some training in cooking and table service. This sounds like a strenuous program. In reality it seemed play to girls accustomed to laboring long hours in mill and field.[84]

It was common for older school-age white children to work in the textile mills during the day. Therefore, the primary reason most young women left school early was financial. In lieu of tuition, Gray's first Opportunity School accepted country donations of potatoes, beans, corn, flour, and eggs, and she supplemented expenses with contributions from volunteer teachers and the South Carolina Illiteracy Commission. The following year, Lander College, a school for white females located in Greenwood, South Carolina, served as the site for the Opportunity School, which enrolled white females over sixteen years who had not completed more than the fifth grade. Ninety enrolled; two were from towns, nine were from the country, and seventy-nine were from cotton mills. In her Lander report Gray noted:

> In an effort to get the message of the Opportunity School to those in their communities who had been deprived of an education, for we realized that the class we wished to reach did not read the papers and only through personal influence, financial assistance, and encouragement of friends could they be persuaded to leave home.[85]

In succeeding summers, various colleges in the state donated their campuses for the one-month session of the school and the numbers of enrollment continued to increase. For example, the following year after the first session, 89 students attended the Opportunity School at Lander College; and by 1923, there were 180 students and three locations at Tamassee, Lander, and Erskine College.[86] The needs of adult white males would eventually shape the program, especially in the creation of an all-year school in 1947, but the needs of females were most important to Gray in the 1920s and the 1930s.

Overtly, the curriculum included instruction in reading, writing, arithmetic, spelling, health habits, civics, good manners, domestic science (including hygiene), and arts and crafts work. The hidden curriculum constituted important dimensions of Wil Lou Gray's life experience and reform impulses grounded in her Methodist upbringing. For example, although the main emphasis was on teaching illiterate or near-illiterate females reading, writing, and basic arithmetic, the underlying virtues of faith in God and country were evident in the curricular focus on introducing young women to middle-class concepts of culture, including religion, morals, manners, etiquette, and citizenship. Style, etiquette, and manners, especially table manners, also constituted important elements of the original Opportunity School program.

According to Gray, "The schools' courses are built on life's needs to take them from wherever they are and lead them to wherever they can go."[87] In one summer month, Gray managed to introduce women of the mills and farms to middle-class culture. Meal times were formal occasions where women practiced formal speech and proper manners.[88] Moreover, as in the religious revivalist rhetoric familiar in the work of Cora Wilson Stewart, Gray's work had elements of a holy crusade. Indeed, she made scripture an integral part of Opportunity School daily activities. The religious emphasis is evident in the evening Vespers Services and the Bible reading lessons of the curriculum.[89]

The annual publication *The Open Door* chronicled the ideals, efforts, achievements, and curriculum of the Opportunity Schools. The first issue, published in 1929, detailed a day-by-day account of the college and the curriculum, including demonstrations of good table manners, a program of singing songs such as "Home Sweet Home," and evening prayers.[90] Group photographs in volume one of *The Open Door* documented various clubs, composed of both white male and white female students, under headings such as "Good Citizenship Club," "Good Manners Club," and the

"Better English Club."[91] In addition to academic training, vocational skills such as woodworking, painting, ceramics, and similar crafts and trades were taught at the school to enable students to earn a living.

The Opportunity Schools made it possible for many whites to complete the equivalency of a high school diploma, and Gray was instrumental in implementing the first standardized tests for high school graduation. Later, Erskine College offered a summer session for white males. The advance publicity bulletin read:

> For years institutions have offered summer courses to the educated—teachers, ministers, and doctors—but this summer the doors of a college will be thrown wide open to the neglected and forgotten men of the mill, the farm, and the home, in order that life for them might be made easier, happier, and more useful.[92]

Eventually, Gray attempted to establish educational programs for African Americans. For example, she began an "Opportunity School for Negroes" at Seneca Junior College in 1931 and another at Voorhees Industrial School in 1936.[93] Similar to her curriculum for white students of the mill villages, at Voorhees, African American students remodeled a dilapidated four-room tenant house for the purpose of teaching students "how to make the most of the materials at hand."[94] While engaged in this project, students not only learned the 3 Rs, but also thrift, economy, and sanitary living conditions, as well as the social possibilities of a home.[95] In 1938 Gray arranged an Opportunity School for 72 African Americans from 25 counties at Benedict College, in Columbia, South Carolina, in cooperation with the W.P.A. Education Division.[96]

Wil Lou Gray's persona and character is of a dual nature. On the one hand, she was in sync with the mill owners themselves, "attempting at once to tame the 'wild' unruly lower classes and provide for a more efficient labor force."[97] On the other hand, she was determined to free working-class poor and people of color from economic tyranny. Key to understanding her work is knowing that she understood the problems of poverty and illiteracy to be inextricably linked with race, class, and gender. Moreover, she understood that for the citizens of South Carolina to reach a higher standard of living, strong leadership in the area of adult illiteracy was imperative. Although leadership was not easy when working within established bureaucratic systems, Gray used face-to-face persistence as the approach that enabled her to effectively lobby for her cause.

Gray sidestepped the obstacles without reconceptualizing them. For instance, when she was told that the state would not pay anyone connected with the Opportunity School unless they were a teacher, she solicited funds through her connections with Baptist churches or women's clubs to pay for house mothers and nurses. Her desire to provide broader social services within her schools indicates her realization that schools were connected to the larger community.

By performing public service in the form of teaching, Gray moved beyond traditional domestic gender roles without challenging the gender hierarchy. As a rural school teacher, faculty member in a women's college, supervisor for rural schools, and supervisor of adult education, she filled positions deemed acceptable for women. Although she moved beyond traditional class boundaries by helping to pick cotton, plant and harvest seed potatoes, and clean outhouses in order to get her schools started, she did not challenge class boundaries.

There is evidence however, that Gray was aware of the constraints placed upon her as a woman, particularly concerning the reward structure within the state educational bureaucracy, as when she reminded:

> You see I am just a woman; and regardless of training, twelve months active work, and long hours running into the night, I am not worth what men are to the state. Twenty years from now that will not be the case, but that is the penalty I must pay for being born in the early eighties.[98]

Gray sought to use education as an instrument for social and economic uplift for working class women from farms and mills, focusing on exposing her students to middle-class culture in an effort to empower them. While they may have gained some insights into middle-class morality, good manners, and proper English grammar, her efforts did not significantly alter their status or income.

Throughout her career, Gray demonstrated a consistent pattern of indirect but assertive leadership. Like Stewart, she was a pioneer in attacking the problems of adult illiteracy, and she saw—years before a number of political leaders in South Carolina saw—that it was impossible for the state to move forward as long as large numbers of people were strangled by illiteracy and poverty. Unlike Stewart, Gray was concerned with illiterate African Americans as well as whites. She worked to make programs available to adult citizens of South Carolina regardless of their race, class, or gender. Although Gray's efforts in adult education were mainly concentrated on working-class poor white Americans, she warned legislators and educators that illiteracy was also a problem among African Americans and that adequate state funding needed to be appropriated for southern blacks.

Wil Lou Gray and Cora Wilson Stewart shared a common struggle to combat adult illiteracy among whites in the South by building an infrastructure of schools and public policy initiatives. A testimonial to the mutual affection they had for each other is evidenced in a signed and dedicated copy of Stewart's book, *Moonlight Schools,* in which the author writes, "To my valiant comrade Wil Lou Gray from Cora Wilson Stewart, Frankfort, Ky. Jan. 30, 1923."[99]

Annie Webb Blanton: Taking on Texas and the Nation

Annie Webb Blanton (1870–1945) was a teacher, a suffragist, and the first woman in Texas elected to statewide office. Born in Houston, she was one of seven children of Thomas Lindsay and

Eugenia (Webb) Blanton. Her twin sister Fannie, died as a girl. A brother, Thomas Lindsay Blanton, represented central west Texas in the United States Congress from 1917 to 1936.[100] Like Cora Wilson Stewart and Wil Lou Gray, Blanton was raised in a family of adequate means and was exposed early to the advantages of education. She attended school in Houston and LaGrange. After graduating from La Grange High School in 1886, she taught in both elementary and secondary schools.

Later, Blanton attended the University of Texas, graduating in 1899. She then moved to Denton, Texas, to serve on the English faculty of North Texas State Normal College (now the University of North Texas), 1901–1918.[101] In Denton, she became active in the Texas State Teachers Association quickly exemplifying her own belief that white women of her social and economic class and profession were capable of improving society and reforming schools. She also was instrumental in founding the City Federation of Women's Clubs in Denton and took a leading role in the town's Women's Shakespeare Club.[102] Blanton actively participated in and benefited from the organized efforts of these clubs, and she understood, as historian Anne Firor Scott later wrote, that "the power of association had its own inner dynamic."[103]

Blanton's experience also demonstrated the translation of women's club work into larger realms, as further described by Scott:

> Women learned how to conduct business, carry on meetings, speak in public, and manage money. Experiences in small-scale voluntary associations prepared women for politics broadly defined. By finding a way to take up public concerns, they were contributing to the expansion of American democracy, first indirectly and then in 1920, directly.[104]

Undoubtedly, Blanton's experiences in women's club leadership came into play when she was elected president of the Texas State Teachers Association in 1916, the first woman to hold this position.

In February 1918, women obtained the right to vote in Texas primaries. Governor William P. Hobby, himself a suffragist supporter, asked Blanton to run for state superintendent of public instruction. In the July 1918 primary, when Texas women exercised their voting rights for the first time, Blanton defeated incumbent Walter F. Doughty and Brandon Trussell by a large margin.[105] Her victory in the general election in November made her the first woman in Texas elected to statewide office.[106]

As state superintendent, Blanton became aware of the discrimination against women and began a lifelong effort to unite competent, experienced women teachers in a struggle against professional unfairness and a commitment to use their talents for social betterment. During her four-year tenure as state superintendent, she established a system of free textbooks, revised teacher certification laws, raised teacher's salaries, and initiated efforts to improve rural education. In 1920 voters passed her proposed Better Schools Amendment which was designed to remove constitutional limitations on tax rates for local school districts.

Blanton gave up her chance for another term as state superintendent to run unsuccessfully for the United States Congress in 1922.[107] Subsequently, she returned to the University of Texas, received her master's degree, and began a career as a professor of education at the same institution. Except for a leave of absence to earn a Ph.D. from Cornell University, she remained a professor of education there for the rest of her life. She became an expert in rural education training and was especially interested in the needs of rural schools.

While teaching at the University of Texas throughout the 1920s, Blanton began to form ideas for a network of competent female colleagues. She recalled that while she served as state superintendent a man told her that women's inability to stand together was hurting the teaching profession and the quality of education in Texas.[108] She also recognized that teachers throughout the country were plagued by low salaries, limited opportunities for advancement, and pressure to resign upon marriage. Recognizing these problems as gender biased, she began to consider the possibility of an honorary society for women educators as a means of uniting selected teachers to address barriers that limited professional opportunities and raise professional standards within the highly feminized profession.[109] In 1929 Blanton founded Delta Kappa Gamma, now an international society for women educators.[110]

In 1936, when the organization was seven years old, Blanton wrote:

> The Founders were strongly of the opinion that an organized body of women teachers selected from among the best in the profession united by bonds of friendship and by the force of common purposes—for the betterment of women teachers and the improvement of schools generally—would have an opportunity for rendering real service to education.[111]

From 1929 until her death in 1945, Blanton dominated Delta Kappa Gamma and through it her national reputation in education increased.[112]

Blanton published several books during her career, including *Review Outline and Exercises in English Grammar* (1903), *A Handbook of Information as to Education in Texas* (1922), *Advanced English Grammar* (1928), and *The Child of the Texas One-Teacher School* (1936).[113] Besides the Delta Kappa Gamma Society, she was also active in national education groups and served as vice president in the National Education Association in 1917, 1919, and 1921.[114]

Upon her death, Blanton's colleagues remarked that she had always had been a "firm believer in the efficiency of organization as an instrument for progress."[115] She recognized the value of organizations and associations throughout the 1920s; and while teaching at the University of Texas, she planned a white woman's organization that would be based on her involvement in club work but that contained a professional, rather than a political, patriotic or literary emphasis.[116] Similar to the American Association of University Women, Delta Kappa Gamma was designed to address the needs of professional white women and provide a sisterhood for educators from the elementary to the college level.[117] By including in her new organization women from all levels of teaching, Blanton envisioned a distinguished group of educators whose joint efforts would result in both increased opportunities and long-overdue recognition for women teachers.[118]

Similar to Blanton, one liberal teacher, Sara Towles Reed, in a very conservative New Orleans, fought for better schools, better working conditions, and better salaries for her female counterparts over the course of her forty-year career. Her crusade was inspired by her own dismissal as a teacher in 1921,when her secret marriage became public upon her husband's death. Reed then enrolled in night classes at Loyola Law School. After earning a law degree in three years, she remained in the teaching profession and became the dominant force in New Orleans' teachers associations. She did not hesitate to confront those in power—principals, superintendents, or the governor. Like Blanton, she worked for gender equity and used teachers' associations as vehicles for gaining intellectual and economic advances for men and women. She succeeded in receiving equal pay for women teachers.

Similarly, Annie Webb Blanton sought to remove barriers that limited the professional opportunities of women teachers. She established close professional ties with competent female colleagues and recognized that such women were a potentially powerful group if they could be organized.[119] According to Cottrell:

> A key to understanding Delta Kappa Gamma and Blanton's involvement in it lies in recognizing her consistency in showing little direct interest in women who planned to teach only briefly, women who were unwilling to work hard, or women who were not of her own class and race.[120]

Blanton never married and acted as surrogate mother to the Delta Kappa Gamma organization. She dedicated her life to what she saw as a noble cause—furthering the interests of white women in the teaching profession

The contributions of Annie Webb Blanton are fixed in Texas educational history, and some consider her the most influential Texas woman educator of the early twentieth century.[121] Public schools are named for her in Austin, Dallas, and Odessa, and a woman's dormitory at the University of Texas at Austin bears her name.[122] She worked during a time when reform and elitism coexisted; and, therefore, it is not surprising that her focus furthering the interests of white women went unquestioned by progressive leaders in the field of education. She lived and worked in a white middle-class Texas world and did not endeavor or desire to extend her professional efforts beyond it.

Legacies in Context

Born in the American South when it confronted the last days of the Reconstruction era, Cora Wilson Stewart, Wil Lou Gray, and Annie Webb Blanton confronted politically Republican themes for schooling. One of the key themes was a preference for powerful central governmental authorities. Stewart, Gray, and Blanton did indeed struggle within the confines of these large bureaucratic systems to build coalitions among marginalized groups. They sought to change systems through the policy process, a task that required them to navigate the terrain of both politics and bureaucracies.

Another Republican theme was to establish at least some educational opportunities for all citizens, not just those who were white or economically advantaged. With the exception of Gray, whose efforts were aimed toward social and economic meliorism for individuals and groups with a history of isolation and disenfranchisement, these women did not work to include African Americans or economically disadvantaged in their educational reform efforts. They understood that few white southerners were eager to see blacks educated or to see their taxes spent on schools for African Americans. While the Republicans after the Civil War urged increased taxation to support public schools, traditional white southerners were suspicious of any state-enforced education system that used their money to potentially threaten their social order.

The systems thinkers described here supported educational reform struggles for better programs to deal with a new agenda of social problems including poverty, domestic abuse, child abuse, poor sanitation, widespread epidemics of disease, adult illiteracy, and the social consequences of alcoholism and excessive drinking. However, they were careful to exhibit non-alienating approaches that demonstrated their desire to improve the existing systems without attempting to overthrow them. In short, they challenged male dominance in politics and education by being pro-woman without being anti-man.

Although the word "feminist" was not in their vocabulary, these systems thinkers found their motivation in a naturally developing awareness of gender inequities. Although their efforts were sometimes limited by narrowing their approaches to recognize the difficulties they confronted, they managed to leave indelible marks on the shape of southern education policies and practices.

CHAPTER SIX

Conclusions: Intersections of the Mind and Heart

The reform impulse of the Progressive Era offered women unusual opportunities to move from private to public spheres, to achieve professional prominence, and to contribute to social betterment causes. Work in education, in particular, "served as leverage for some women to live their lives as agents of change."[1] In the South and in the realm of education, those opportunities for women were enlarged by the great needs in areas ranging from adult literacy and schooling for African Americans to compulsory attendance and administrative efficiency. To a large extent, educational needs were perceived as closely allied with child welfare and social services causes and, therefore, allowed women acceptable career venues outside the home. Additionally, efforts that would aim at "reform" in the South could range widely in a region where concepts of progressivism were not narrowed by reference to specific professional practices. The women of this study were, therefore, able to initiate substantial accomplishments while guided more by intuition and circumstance than by professional training or understanding.

Nevertheless, these women needed to draw on great reservoirs of energy and commitment in order to undertake their reform work. Their struggles for resources and serious regard were constant and exhausting. In most cases, they were assisted by a fairly selfless sense of cause; and, in many cases, they were further supported by deep religious faith and spiritual nourishment. The reform impulse was an appropriate match for evangelical sense of purpose.

A Special Brand of Progressive Reform

Typically, the women in our study approached educational reform in very intuitive and focused ways. They so readily accepted the popular connection between education and a better life that they often failed to ponder the larger curricular, sociological, or pedagogical elements of that education. Rather, they quickly focused on selected and discrete issues, groups, or institutions and were determined to improve the lives of illiterate adults, mill workers, African Americans, Appalachian poor, teachers, or others. There is little indication that these women interpreted their educational work within a larger scope of social change, although the African American women of our study may have come closest to this larger view by perceiving racial uplift as part of their mission. The educational work of all the women in this study can be viewed more appropriately as a subset of social progressivism, than a subset of educational progressivism.

To some extent, their narrowing focus removed these women from some large and important social issues like cyclical rural poverty or equal rights for women and blacks. Their mission was not to change the social order, but to spark better opportunities and better practices within that order. Thus, while they supported conceptions of democracy and social justice, their work was circumscribed by the reality of local and pressing needs. They generally worked with the problems and people most immediate to their own experience and observation. Of the women we studied, only Annie Webb Blanton appeared to adopt a wider and longer lens on educational issues, but even her work was mediated by narrow conceptions of race and class boundaries.

Interestingly, our findings about the nature of the progressive impulse among the women educators we studied do not completely agree with interpretations of analysts who assert that southern progressives in general "saw education as a means of improving society" and aimed educational efforts at citizens who would be "trained to meet the needs of the New South."[2] Nor do our observations share the emphasis of analysts who find southern progressive reforms lodged in administrative and institutional priorities undertaken by groups that ranged from school improvement leagues to coalitions pushing for consolidated schools.[3] Instead, we view the work of the women we have presented as fairly opportunistic and pragmatic-sparked by a larger environment of social contribution and evangelical commitment, but aimed more toward improved individual lives than institutional or societal change. For some, education was the means to acquiring cultural capital within the existing system, but did not necessarily translate to empowerment to change the system.

It would be easy to conclude that these southern women educators were thinking too small to be considered "reformers." However, while their efforts may not have tackled reform as social change head on, they certainly could be viewed as elements that demonstrated effective practices within that change. As such, they managed to mark niches within the region where reformist endeavors could coexist with long-standing patterns of elitism, racism, and sexism.

A Gendered Experience

The experiences of the women we have presented support the idea of multiple dimensions for active women of the Progressive Era who walked a thin line of acceptance between the activities of a competent professional and the behavior of a southern lady. Robyn Muncy referred to this dilemma as "a combination of autonomy and circumscription" and found that for women working for progressive causes in the early twentieth century "prescriptions for female behavior directly contradicted the solidifying requirement of professional conduct."[4]

The slowly changing circumstances of southern women in the early twentieth century may have foreshadowed a burgeoning new woman, but the traditional ideal of a lady on a pedestal was still alive and well. Politicians still floated the notion of "the purity and sanctity of our womanhood" in defense of lynching policies as late as 1935, and men in general asserted patriarchal privilege in decision making outside the domestic sphere.[5] Thus, feminine educational leaders confronted little hospitality in a highly gendered realm. Unlike their progressive counterparts working in areas such as child welfare or civic beautification, women working in education treaded on conflicted ground. While teaching was acceptable as woman's work, administrative leadership and policy-making were not.

The women we studied did not directly confront sexism, but rather used varying approaches at varying times to work within a gendered environment. Frequently, they found that their ability to succeed depended on defeminizing factors. For example, most did not have traditional marriages or family lives; and many did little to establish female physical attractiveness regarding their bodies or their dress. Yet, when necessary, Martha Berry or Charlotte Hawkins Brown could call on personal femininity to get a foot in the door to the man's world of finance or foundations. Mary McLeod Bethune and Lucy Laney could draw upon the image of nurturing matriarch; and even Wil Lou Gray could appear as amusing gadfly who talked state legislators into agreement by sheer persistence.

Thus, the women of this study did not actually challenge gender norms or view themselves as feminists, although they made some progress toward feminist ideologies as role models and accomplished professionals. If they displayed any inclination toward feminism at all, it was a strategic feminism that allowed them to selectively and alternately adopt postures that seemed nurturing, sweet, professional, and/or persistent. Just as they made room for the coexistence of socioeconomic elitism and progressivism, they also found that their reform efforts could work within constraints of sexism. Undoubtedly, however, as Crocco,et al. found about northern female progressive educators, "their authority was continually undercut by their status as women."[6]

The African American women we studied did grasp a larger social scope of endeavor in terms of racial equality. Ranging from Nannie Helen Burroughs involvement in antilynching campaigns to Mary McLeod Bethune's work for black youth in the National Youth Administration, the voices of these women were heard beyond their immediate education efforts to include the push for uplift of their race. Yet, in their educational work, they treaded carefully in terms of racial issues, often overemphasizing the extent to which their aims suited elite white notions of training blacks only in vocational work and discipline.

When Glazer and Slater studied women in academic, medical, and scientific professions during the Progressive Era, they determined that those who succeeded adopted one or more of four strategies for asserting their abilities in a public sphere and a man's world: superperformance, separatism, subordination, and innovation. Of these, the southern women educators could best be viewed as "superperformers" who "sought professional status through extraordinary efforts and performance" and who "overcame barriers by dint of hard work, outstanding ability, and their willingness to sacrifice traditional relationships for their careers."[7] In some cases, these educators also could be seen as "innovators" who "tended to remove themselves from direct competition with male professionals" by locating their efforts in isolated locations (e.g., Alice Lloyd in Appalachia) or by selecting substantive areas ignored by men (e.g., Cora Wilson Stewart and schools for adult literacy).[8] None of our women strictly qualified as separatists (working only with women) or as subordinates (filling positions below men in a hierarchy).

In addition to influences related to being female and being southern, for many of these women another prominent influence was their religious devotion. Time and time again, many of them were able to persist because of a sense that a higher being was calling them. And in turn, they were determined to include religious discipline and piety in their own teachings. Undoubtedly, their determination to embrace and teach a life of spiritual obedience helped them to reconcile their much lesser obedience to traditional southern female patterns of marriage and family and traditional notions of the private sphere as the appropriate venue for women's activities.

We view the work and lives of these women we studied as somewhat paradoxical, sometimes difficult to interpret. They accomplished much with multiple motivations and means, always testing the parameters of the norms that restricted their professional lives. Few common threads mark their experiences because there were as yet no common routes to accomplishment for southern women. Each woman who played a major role toward educational progress worked separately to discover how to accommodate without subordinating and achieve without overstepping. Perhaps the most pervasive common thread among these women was the energy, commitment, and persistence they brought to an intuited notion that education was at the heart of opportunity in the South of the Progressive Era.

Notes

Preface

1. Joseph F. Kett, "Women and the Progressive Impulse," in *The Web of Southern Social Relations: Women, Family, and Education*, Walter J. Fraser, Jr., R. Frank Saunders, Jr., and Jon L. Wakelyn, eds. (Athens, GA: The University of Georgia Press, 1985), 174.

2. Penina Migdal Glazer and Miriam Slater, *Unequal Colleagues: The Entrance of Women into the Professions, 1890–1940* (New Brunswick: Rutgers University Press, 1987), 210.

3. Anne Firor Scott, *Making the Invisible Woman Visible* (Urbana, IL: University of Illinois Press, 1984), 2.

4. Anne Firor Scott, "Unfinished Business," in *Taking Off the White Gloves: Southern Women and Women Historians*, Michele Gillespie and Catherine Clinton, eds. (Columbia, MO: University of Missouri Press, 1998), 119.

5. Kett, "Women and the Progressive Impulse," 166.

6. Margaret Smith Crocco, Petra Munro, and Kathleen Weiler, *Pedagogies of Resistance: Women Educator Activists, 1880–1960* (New York: Teachers College Press, 1999), 3.

7. Sari Bicklen, *School Work: Gender and the Cultural Construction of Teaching* (New York: Teachers College Press, 1995).

8. Anastatia Sims, *The Power of Femininity in the New South* (Columbia, SC: University of South Carolina Press, 1997).

9. Amy Thompson McCandless, The Past in the Present: Women's Higher Education in the Twentieth Century American South (Tuscaloosa: University of Alabama Press, 1999).

10. Robyn Muncy, *Creating a Female Dominion in American Reform, 1890–1935* (New York: Oxford University Press, 1991).

11. Glazer and Slater, *Unequal Colleagues*; Joanne V. Hawks and Mary C. Ellis, "Heirs of the Southern Progressive Tradition: Women in Southern Legislatures in the 1920s," in *Southern Women*, Carolyn Matheny Dillman, ed. (New York: Hemisphere Publishing, 1988); and Anne Goodwyn Jones, *Tomorrow Is Another Day: The Woman Writer in the South, 1850–1936* (Baton Rouge: Louisiana State University Press, 1981).

Chapter One

1. See, for example, Peter G. Filene, "An Obituary for the Progressive Movement," *American Quarterly*, 22 (Spring 1970), 20–33; and Jeffrey E. Mirel, "Progressive School Reform in Comparative Perspective," in *Southern Cities, Southern Schools: Public Education in the Urban South*, David N. Plank and Rick Ginsberg, eds. (New York: Greenwood, 1990), 151–76.

2. See, for example, Edward Krug, *The Shaping of the American High School, 1880–1920* (Madison: University of Wisconsin Press, 1964); and David B. Tyack, *The One Best System: A History of American Urban Education* (Cambridge: Harvard University Press, 1974).
3. Filene, "An Obituary," 30.

4. Herbert M. Kliebard, *The Struggle for the American Curriculum, 1893–1958*, 2nd ed. (New York: Routledge, 1995), 243.

5. Mirel, "Progressive School Reform," 151.

6. Wilbur J. Cash, *The Mind of the South* (New York: Alfred Knopf, 1941), viii.

7. Edgar W. Knight, "Some Economic, Political and Social Inflences on Education in the South," in *Secondary Education in the South*, W. Carson Ryan, J. Minor Gwynn, Arnold K. King, eds. (Chapel Hill: University of North Carolina Press, 1946), 4.

8. William A. Link, *The Rebuilding of Old Commonwealths* (Boston: St. Martin's, 1996), xii.

9. Gerald W. Johnson, "Critical Attitudes North and South," in *The Journal of Social Forces*, May, 1924, 43.

10. Knight, "Some Influences," 4.

11. Stuart G. Noble, "Education of the Negro," in *Twenty-Five Years of American Education*, I.L. Kandel, ed. (Freeport, NY: Books for Libraries, 1924), 406.

12. Joseph F. Kett, "Women and the Progressive Impulse in Southern Education," in *The Web of Southern Social Relations: Women, Family and Education* (Athens, GA: The University of Georgia Press, 1985), 171.

13. Robert A. Margo, *Race and Schooling in the South, 1880–1950: An Economic History* (Chicago: University of Chicago Press, 1990), 7.

14. Cash, The Mind of the South, 218.

15. Dewey W. Grantham, *Southern Progressivism: The Reconciliation of Progress and Tradition* (Knoxville: University of Kentucky Press, 1983), 276.

16. G. S. Dickerman, "The South Compared to the North in Educational Requirements," in *Proceedings of the Fourth Conference for Education in the South,* Winston-Salem, NC, 18–20 April 1901, 15.

17. Russell Sage Foundation, *A Comparative Study of Public School Systems in the Forty-Eight States* (New York: Russell Sage Foundation, 1912), 11.

18. Knight, "Some Influences," 14.

19. Russell Sage Foundation, *A Comparative Study,* 3.

20. Marcia E. Turner, "Black School Politics in Atlanta, Georgia, 1909–1943," in *Southern Cities, Southern Schools: Public Education in the Urban South,* David N. Plank and Rick Ginsberg, eds. (New York: Greenwood, 1990), 177–97.

21. Howard N. Rabinwitz, "Continuity and Change: Southern Urban Development, 1860–1900," in eds., Brownell and Goldfield, *The City in Southern History*, 112.

22. Russell Sage Foundation, *A Comparative Study*, 19.

23. Ibid., 23.

24. Margo, *Race and Schooling*, 54; Russell Sage Foundation, *A Comparative Study*, 19.

25. For demographic detail and analysis of the period, see Howard W. Odum, *Southern Regions of the United States* (Chapel Hill: University of North Carolina Press, 1936) and Gerald Johnson, *The Wasted Land* (Chapel Hill: University of North Carolina Press, 1937).

26. Edgar W. Knight, "Education in the South," in *Twenty-Five Years of American Education*, I.L. Kandel, ed. (Freeport, NY: Books for Libraries, 1924), 395.

27. Johnson, *The Wasted Land*, 55.

28. Arthur S. Link, "The Progressive Movement in the South," in *North Carolina Historical Review*, xxiii, 2 (April), 1946, 173.

29. Ibid., 194.

30. Noble, "Education of the Negro," 415.

31. C. Vann Woodward, *Origins of the New South*, 1877–1913 (Baton Rouge: Louisiana State University Press, 1951), 369.

32. David B. Tyack, *Turning Points in American Education* (Waltham, MA: Blaisdell Publishing, 1967), 268; William A. Link, *The Rebuilding of Old Commonwealths* (Boston: St. Martin's, 1996), 110.

33. Margo, *Race and Schooling*, 44–48.

34. James D. Anderson, *Education of Blacks in the South, 1860–1935* (Chapel Hill: University of North Carolina Press, 1988), 97.

35. See, for economic arguments related to education for southern black citizens, Margo, *Race and Schooling*.

36. Anderson, *Education of Blacks*, 241.

37. W. H. Plemmons, "Extension and Equalization of Educational Opportunity in the South," in *Secondary Education in the South*, W. Carson Ryan, J. Minor Gwynn, Arnold K. King, eds. (Chapel Hill: University of North Carolina Press, 1946), 20–36.

38. These and other examples of institutionalized inequalities can be found in Anderson, *Education of Blacks*, 190–96; Turner, "Black School Politics," 180–95; and Tyack, *Turning Points*, 269.

39. David N. Plank, "Why Study the South?" in *Southern Cities, Southern Schools: Public Education in the Urban South*, David N. Plank and Rick Ginsberg, eds. (New York: Greenwood, 1990), 4.

40. Gerald W. Johnson, "Critical Attitudes North and South," in *The Journal of Social Forces* (May), 1924, 577.

41. Jack Temple Kirby, *Darkness at the Dawning: Race and Reform in the Progressive South* (New York: J.B. Lippincott, 1972), 4.

42. George S. Counts, "Dare Progressive Education Be Progressive?" in *Progressive Education*, ix (1932), 258.

43. Tyack, *The One Best System*; Mirel, "Progressive School Reform," 157.

44. Dewey W. Grantham, *Southern Progressivism: The Reconciliation of Progress and Tradition* (Knoxville: University of Tennessee Press, 1983), 246; Woodward, Origins, 401.

45. Grantham, *Southern Progressivism*, 231.

46. See, for example, Mirel, "Progressive School Reform."

47. See Philip N. Racine, "Public Education in the New South: A School System for Atlanta, 1868–1879," in *Southern Cities*, Plank and Ginsberg, eds. (New York: Greenwood Press, 1990), 37–58, and Turner, "Black School Politics."

48. Anderson, *Education of Blacks*, 237.

49. Joseph F. Kett, "Women and the Progressive Impulse," 166–180.

50. For examples of sentiments concerning child labor, see David L. Carlton, *Mill and Town in South Carolina, 1880–1920* (Baton Rouge: Louisiana State University Press, 1982).

51. Louise A. Allen and Katherine C. Reynolds, "Tenacious Southern Progressives: Confounding Mencken's Myth of Me-

diocrity," paper presented at the annual conference of the American Education Research Association, 1999, Toronto, Canada.

52. Filene, "An Obituary," 22–30.

Chapter Two

1. Simone de Beauvoir, *The Second Sex*. (New York: Knopf, 1949; Eng. Trans., 1964). Beauvoir shows how women have occupied a secondary position in history, much like that of an oppressed and exploited minority, because of social conditions that have denied their potential.

2. For further discussion of Progressivism in the South, see Anne Firor Scott, *The Southern Lady: From Pedestal to Politics, 1830–1930* (Chicago: University of Chicago Press, 1970).; Anastatia Sims, *The Power of Femininity in the New South: Women's Organizations and Politics in North Carolina, 1880–1930* (Columbia, SC: The University of South Carolina Press, 1997); Jean E. Friedman, *The Enclosed Garden: Women and Community in the Evangelical South, 1830–1900* (Chapel Hill, NC: The University of North Carolina Press, 1985); and Dewey Grantham, *Southern Progressivism: The Reconciliation of Progress and Tradition* (Knoxville, TN: The University of Tennessee Press, 1983).

3. Joseph F. Kett, "Women and the Progressive Impulse in Southern Education" in ed. Walter Fraser, Jr., *The Web of Southern Social Relations* (Athens, GA: University of Georgia Press, 1985), 166.

4. Kett, "Women and the Progressive Impulse," 166.

5. Friedman, *The Enclosed Garden*, 6.

6. Scott, *The Southern Lady*.

7. Ibid., 234.

8. Ibid., xi.

9. Ibid., xi.

10. Ibid., 284.

11. Maxine Schwartz Seller (editor), *Women Educators in the United States 1820–1993: A Bio-Bibliographical Sourcebook.* Westport, CT: Greenwood, 1994), xv.

12. Robyn Muncy, *Creating a Female Dominion in American Reform: 1890–1935* (New York: Oxford University Press, 1991).

13. Ibid., 3.

14. Ibid.

15. Amy Thompson McCandless, *The Past in the Present: Women's Higher Education in the Twentieth-Century American South* (Tuscaloosa, AL: The University of Alabama Press, 1999).

16. Sochen, *Herstory*, 234.

17. Ibid., 234.

18. Ibid., 250.

19. Spring, *The American School,* 78.

20. Kliebard, *The Struggle,* 90.

21. Debbie Mauldin Cottrell, *Pioneer Woman Educator: The Progressive Spirit of Annie Webb Blanton* (College Station, TX: Texas A&M University Press, 1993).

22. Cottrell, *Pioneer Woman,* 5.

23. Spring, *The American School,* 139–140.

24. Ibid., 139–140.

25. Seller, *Women Educators,* 49.

26. Sims, *The Power of Femininity,* 95.

27. Ibid., 95.

28. Ibid., 95.

29. For further discussion of the "cult of true womanhood," see Muncy, *Creating a Female.*

30. John S. Brubacher and Willis Rudy, *Higher Education in Transition: A History of American Colleges and Universities,* 1636-1976 (New York: Harper & Row Publishers, 1976)., 35.

31. Ibid., 46.

32. Elizabeth Minnich, Jean O'Barr, and Rachel Rosenfeld, *Restructuring the Academy: Women's Education and Women's Studies* (Chicago: The University of Chicago Press, 1988)..

33. Brubacher and Rudy, *Higher Education,* 46.

34. Scott, *The Southern Lady.* The controversy of an employed woman stepping out of her domestic sphere became less relevant in the face of an overwhelming need for labor. This was especially true in the beleaguered South where widows and their daughters often managed family properties.

35. Minnich et al., *Restructuring the Academy.* Although opponents viewed university education for women as a direct challenge to the traditional place of women in American society, many pioneering women managed to persevere in the face of hostility, uncertainty, and insecurity.

36. Brubacher and Rudy, *Higher Education.*

37. Minnich et al., *Restructuring the Academy.*

38. Brubacher and Rudy, *Higher Education.*

39. Minnich et al., *Restructuring the Academy.*

40. Brubacher and Rudy, *Higher Education.*

41. Ibid., 104.

42. Ibid., 108.

43. Amy Thompson McCandless, *The Past in the Present: Women's Higher Education in the Twentieth-Century American South* (Tuscaloosa, AL: The University of Alabama Press, 1999), 89.

44. Leslie Gale Parr, *A Will of Her Own: Sarah Towles Reed and the Pursuit of Democracy in Southern Public Education* (Athens, GA: The University of Georgia Press, 1998), 3.

45. Olga Skorapa, "Mary McLeod Bethune" in Seller, *Women Educators*, 47–55.

46. Scott, *The Southern Lady*, 122–23.

47. David Forgacs, *The Antonio Gramsci Reader: Selected Writings 1916–1935* (New York: New York University Press, 1999).

48. William A. Link, *The Paradox of Southern Progressivism, 1880-1930* (Chapel Hill, NC: The University of North Carolina Press, 1992), 299.

49. For further discussion of the evangelical community and the resulting neighborhood kinship patterns of black and white southern women see Jean Friedman, *The Enclosed Garden* (1985).

50. Norfleet Hardy, *Farm, Mill, and Classroom: A History of Tax Supported Adult Education in South Carolina to 1960* (Columbia, SC: The University of South Carolina, 1967).

51. June Sochen, *Herstory: A Woman's View of American History* (New York: Alfred Publishing, 1974).

52. For further discussion of social meliorism at the turn of the twentieth century see, Herbert M. Kliebard, *The Struggle for the American Curriculum 1893–1958* (New York: Routledge, 1995); Daniel Tanner and Laurel Tanner, *History of the School Curriculum* (New York: Macmillan, 1990); and Joel Spring, The American School 1642–1985 (New York: Longman, 1986).

53. Dennis Carlson, *Making Progress: Education and Culture in New Times* (New York: Teachers College Press, 1997).

54. Carlson, *Making Progress*.

55. John Dewey, *Democracy and Education: An Introduction to the Philosophy of Education* (New York: Macmillan, 1916).

Chapter Three

1. See, for example, Wayne J. Urban, "History of Education: A Southern Exposure," in *History of Education Quarterly*, Summer, 1981, 131–45; and Edward A. Krug, The Shaping of the American High School (New York: Harper & Row, 1964).

2. William Edward Burghardt DuBois, *The Souls of Black Folk: Essays and Sketches* (Chicago: A.C. McClurg, 1903), 32.

3. Palmer Memorial Institute, "Some Interesting Facts About Our School," recruitment brochure (Sedalia, NC, 1924), 3, Charlotte Eugenia (Hawkins) Brown Papers, 1900–1961, Arthur and Elizabeth Schlesinger Library, Radcliffe College, Cambridge, MA. Microfilm in North Carolina State Division of Archives and History, Raleigh, NC. (Hereafter cited as Brown Papers); Ibid., 1.

4. Louise Daniel Hutchinson, *Anna J. Cooper, A Voice from the South* (Washington, DC: Smithsonian Press, 1981).

5. Marcia G. Synott, "Julia Strudwick Tutwiler," in *Women Educators in the United States, 1820–1993*. Maxine Schwartz Seller, ed. (Westport, CT: Greenwood Press, 1994), 517–524; Caney Junior College Bulletin, 1929, 4, College Catalogs and Bulletins, Archives, Alice Lloyd College, Pippa Passes, KY.

6. Charles W. Wadelington and Richard F. Knapp, *Charlotte Hawkins Brown and Palmer Memorial Institute* (Chapel Hill, NC: University of North Carolina Press, 1999); P. David Searles, *A College for Appalachia: Alice Lloyd on Caney Creek* (Lexington: The University Press of Kentucky, 1995).

7. Synott, "Tutwiler," 518–20.

8. Amy Thompson McCandless, "Elizabeth Avery Colton," in *Women Educators in the United States, 1820–1993*, Maxine Schwartz Seller, ed. (Westport, CT: Greenwood Press, 1994), 152-60; Carolyn Terry Bashaw, Stalwart Women: A Historical Analysis of Deans of Women in the South (New York: Teachers College Press, 1999).

9. Palmer Memorial Institute Charter of Incorporation, November 23, 1907, Brown Papers.

10. Wadelington and Knapp, *Charlotte Hawkins Brown*, 51; Charlotte Hawkins Brown, handwritten notes, N.D., Brown Papers.

11. The complete critical biography of Charlotte Hawkins Brown is Wadelington and Knapp, *Charlotte Hawkins Brown*. See also Tera Hunter, "The Correct Thing: Charlotte Brown and The

Palmer Institute," in *Southern Exposure,* 11, no. 5 (September/October 1983): 37–43; Cecie Jenkins, "The Twig Bender," N.D., typescript in Brown Papers; Constance Hall Marteena, *The Lengthening Shadow of a Woman* (Hicksville, NY: Exposition Press, 1977); Diane Silcox-Jarrett, *Charlotte Hawkins Brown: One Woman's Dream* (Winston-Salem, NC: Bandit Books, 1995); Sandra N. Smith and Earle H. West, "Charlotte Hawkins Brown," in *Journal of Negro Education,* 51, no. 3 (1982), 191–206.

12. Smith and West, "Charlotte Hawkins Brown," 192; Silcox-Jarrett, *Charlotte Hawkins Brown,* 3–5.

13. Charlotte Hawkins Brown, "Some Incidents in the Life of Charlotte Hawkins Brown Growing Out of Racial Situations at the Request of Ralph Bunch," 1937, typescript, 2, Brown Papers.

14. Wadelington and Knapp, *Charlotte Hawkins Brown,* 28.

15. Charlotte Hawkins Brown, "Booker T. Washington's Philosophy of Education and Business," typescript of a speech delivered August 29, 1944, at Negro Men's League, Birmingham, AL, 7, Brown Papers.

16. Brown, "Some Incidents in the Life," 9.

17. Jane Bernard-Powers, "Lucy Craft Laney," in *Women Educators in the United States, 1820–1993.* Maxine Schwartz Seller, ed. (Westport, CT: Greenwood Press, 1994), 276–82; Brown, "Some Incidents in the Life," 9.

18. Marteena, *The Lengthening Shadow,* 11–23; Wadelington and Knapp, *Charlotte Hawkins Brown,* 34–46.

19. Smith and West, "Charlotte Hawkins Brown," 206.

20. Wadelington and Knapp, *Charlotte Hawkins Brown*; Palmer Memorial Institute bulletins, 1924, 1931–32, and 1935–36, Brown Papers.

21. Frances Guthrie to Charlotte Hawkins, N.D., 1907, Brown Papers.

22. Smith and West, "Charlotte Hawkins Brown," 193.

23. Carolyn C. Denard, "Introduction," in Charlotte Hawkins Brown, Mammy: An Appeal to the Heart of the South and The Correct Thing to Do, To Say, To Wear (New York: G.K. Hall, 1995), xxv.

24. Hunter, "The Correct Thing," 39.

25. Smith and West, "Charlotte Hawkins Brown," 199; Wadelington and Knapp, *Charlotte Hawkins Brown*, 63–67.

26. Wadelington and Knapp, *Charlotte Hawkins Brown*, 69–73.

27. Wadelington and Knapp, *Charlotte Hawkins Brown*, 77–79; Marteena, *The Lengthening Shadow*, 18-26.

28. Palmer Memorial Institute bulletins, 1924, 1931–32, Brown Papers.

29. Palmer Memorial Institute bulletin, 1935–36, Brown Papers.

30. Wadelington and Knapp, *Charlotte Hawkins Brown*, 130–31 and 143-55.

31. Galen Stone to Charlotte Hawkins Brown, 25 April 1921, 9 May 1921, Brown Papers.

32. Wadelington and Knapp, *Charlotte Hawkins Brown*, 108.

33. J.S. Ledbetter, "Founder of Alice Freeman Palmer School in North Carolina Challenges White Youth of the South at Berea College," typescript report of speech delivered in 1935, 3, Brown Papers.

34. Charlotte Hawkins Brown, "Some Incidents in the Life of Charlotte Hawkins Brown Growing Out of Racial Situations at the Request of Ralph Bunch," 1937, typescript, 5–7, Brown Papers. In addition to her honorary LL.D. degree from Wilberforce, Brown later received an honorary LL.D. from Lincoln University, an honorary Ed.D. from Howard University, and an honorary Litt.D. from Tuskegee Institute.

35. Palmer Memorial Institute bulletin, 1941, Brown Papers.

36. Denard, "Introduction," iii-v.

37. Ibid., xxxi.

38. Charlotte Hawkins Brown, *The Correct Thing to Do, To Say, To Wear* (New York: Christopher Publishing, 1941), 46.

39. Wadelington and Knapp, *Charlotte Hawkins Brown*, 173–75.

40. Hunter, "The Correct Thing," 40.

41. Joseph Baker, "The Twig Bender of Sedalia," in *The Brown American* (Fall/Winter 1944–45): 10.

42. Griffith Davis, "Finishing School: Wealthiest Families Send Children to Palmer for Polishing," in *Ebony* (October 1947): 23.

43. Marteena, *The Lengthening Shadow*, 47.

44. The only critical biography of Alice Spencer Geddes Lloyd is: P. David Searles, *A College for Appalachia: Alice Lloyd on Caney Creek* (Lexington: The University Press of Kentucky, 1995). See also Carolyn Clay Turner, "Patterns of Educational Initiative, Reorganization and Decline in Eastern Kentucky, 1889–1940: Pikeville Collegiate Institute, Sandy Valley Seminary, and Caney Community Center," Ph.D. dissertation, University of Kentucky-Lexington, 1987.

45. A number of excellent studies shed light retrospectively on the Appalachian region during the Progressive Era, including: Ronald D. Eller, *Miners, Millhands and Mountaineers: Industrialization of the Appalachian South, 1880–1930* (Knoxville: University of Tennessee Press, 1982); John Gaventa, *Power and Powerlessness: Quiescence and Rebellion in an Appalachian* Valley (Urbana: University of Illinois Press, 1980); David Whisnant, Modernizing the Mountaineer (Boone, NC: Appalachian Consortium Press, 1980); and David W. Whisnant, *All That Is Native and Fine: The Politics and Culture in an American Region* (Chapel Hill: University of North Carolina Press, 1983).

46. Whisnant, *All That Is Native*, 48; Searles, *A College for Appalachia*, 79–81. See also, Henry D. Shapiro, *Appalachia On Our Mind: The Southern Mountains and Mountaineers in the American Consciousness, 1870–1920* (Chapel Hill: University of North Carolina Press, 1978).

47. Shapiro, *Appalachia On Oour Mind*, 221–25.

48. Searles, *A College for Appalachia,* 55.

49. Ibid., 19–25. Some accounts ascribe Lloyd's partial paralysis on one side to a case of spinal meningitis either just before or after her marriage. Searles's investigation of her activities at these times demonstrates the likelihood of polio at a slightly earlier time, possibly after her first year at Radcliffe College.

50. For discussions of "new women" and their reform works, see, for example, Arthur Mann, *Yankee Reformers in the Urban Age* (Cambridge: Harvard University Press, 1954) and Rosalind Rosenberg, *Beyond Separate Spheres* (New Haven: Yale University Press, 1982); Searles, A College for Appalachia, 25–31.

51. Searles, *A College for Appalachia,* 34–37; "Four Kentucky Students in Boston on Tour Today," *The Christian Science Monitor* (March 24, 1922): 3.

52. "School in Caney Valley," Time (April 8, 1940): 52; William S. Dutton, "Stay on Stranger," in *The Reader's Digest* (January 1954): 155; Robert W. Sloane, *Alice Lloyd—Boston's Gift to Caney Creek* (Lexington, KY: Thoroughbred Press, 1982): xiii; Jerry C. Davis, *Miracle on Caney Creek* (Lexington, KY: Thoroughbred Press, 1982): 25–26.

53. Sloane, Alice Lloyd, xvi.

54. Searles, *A College for Appalachia,* 53–63; Vera Mae Sloane, What My Heart Wants to Tell (Lexington: University of Kentucky Press, 1987), 108–112.

55. Davis, Miracle on Caney Creek, 37–38.

56. Ibid., 42–52; Searles, A College for Appalachia, 54–58.

57. Davis, Miracle on Caney Creek, 43–44; Searles, *A College for Appalachia,* 60–64.

58. *Caney Junior College Handbook,* 1935–36, Alice Lloyd College Archives.

59. Ibid., 60.

60. Carolyn Clay Turner, *Patterns of Educational Initiative, Reorganization and Decline in Eastern Kentucky, 1889-1940* (Ed.D. Dissertation, University of Kentucky, 1987).

61. Searles, *A College for Appalachia,* 72–79; Turner, *Patterns of Educational Initiative,* 81–82.

62. "Alumni Plan Returns Favor for Little Caney College," *The Hindman (KY) News,* 13 October 1955, 1.

63. Turner, *Patterns of Educational Initiative,* 110–14.

64. Ibid.

65. F.A. Behymer, "Where Illiterate Gave Ground for a College," *St. Louis Post-Dispatch, Everyday Magazine,* 7 December 1941, 1.

66. Sloane, *Alice Lloyd,* 58–59.

67. Searles, *A College for Appalachia,* 82–91.

68. Excellent discussions of the objections to Lloyd and her practices, mostly from other nearby colleges and settlements, are

found in Turner, *Patterns of Educational Initiative,* 160–65, and Searles, *A College for Appalachia,* 120–25.

69. Searles, *A College for Appalachia,* 158–62; Sloane, *Alice Lloyd,* 232–36.

70. There is no critical biography of Martha Berry. See: Anne Firor Scott, "Martha McChesney Berry," in *Notable American Women 1606–1950* (Cambridge: Harvard University Press, 1971), 137–38. Book length memoirs related to Berry and Berry College include Evelyn Hoge Pendley, *A Lady I Loved* (Mt. Berry Georgia: Berry College), 1966.

71. Martha Berry, "Uplifting Backwoods Boys in Georgia," *World's Work,* Vol. 8 (1904), 4986–4992.

72. Today, the Berry College is a fully accredited coeducational comprehensive college with a full range of undergraduate programs and graduate programs in education and business administration.

73. For examples of Martha Berry's approach to donors, see Joyce Blackburn, *Martha Berry: Little Woman With a Big Dream* (New York: J.B. Lippincott, 1968) and Pendley, A Lady I Loved.

74. Blackburn, *Martha Berry,* 108–138; Scott, "Martha McChesney Berry," 138.

Chapter Four

1. For discussions of industrial education, its motivations and impacts concerning race and class, see for example, James

Anderson, *The Education of Blacks in the South 1860–1935* (Chapel Hill: University of North Carolina Press, 1988); W.E.B. DuBois, *Black Reconstruction in America* (New York: Atheneum, 1975); and Theodore R. Mitchell, "From Black to White: The Transformation of Educational Reform in the New South 1890–1910," *Educational Theory* 39(4), Fall 1989, 337–350.

2. See George S. Counts, *Dare the School Build a New Social Order?* (New York: The John Day Co., 1932); John Dewey, *Education and Democracy* (New York: Macmillan, 1916); and, for a comparative overview of manual and industrial training movements, Theodore Lewis, "From Manual Training to Technology Education: The Continuing Struggle to Establish a School Subject in the USA," *Journal of Curriculum Studies* 27(6), 1995, 621–645.

3. The comprehensive biography of Nannie Helen Burroughs is Opal V. Easter, *Nannie Helen Burroughs* (New York: Garland, 1995). See also Earl L. Harrison, *The Dream and the Dreamer* (Washington, D.C.: Nannie H. Burroughs Literature Foundation, 1956).

   Among the many article and book sources for information about Mary McLeod Bethune, the most comprehensive is her biography by Rackham Holt, *Mary McLeod Bethune: A Biography* (Garden City, NY: Doubleday, 1964). See also Audrey Thomas McCluskey and Elaine M. Smith (eds.), *Mary McLeod Bethune, Building a Better World: Essays and Selected Documents* (Bloomington, IN: Indiana University Press, 1999); Florence Johnson Hicks, *Mary McLeod Bethune: Her Own Words of Inspiration* (Washington, DC: Nuclassics and Science Publishing, 1975); and Sheila Y. Flemming, *The Answered Prayer to a Dream,* Bethune-Cookman College, 1904–1994 (Daytona Beach, FL: The Donning Co., 1995).

Janie Porter Barrett information is from Cynthia Neverdon-Morton, "Janie Porter Barrett" in *American National Biography,* Vol. 2, John A. Garraty and Mark C. Carnes, eds. (New York: Oxford University Press, 1999), 232–33.

4. Elaine Smith, "Mary McLeod Bethune Papers: The Bethune-Cookman College Collection, 1922–1955: An Introduction to the Microfilm Edition" (Bethesda, MD: University, 1995), viii.

5. Information about the early life of Nannie Helen Burroughs is from Easter, Nannie Helen Burroughs; Marcia G. Synnott, "Nannie Helen Burroughs," in *Women Educators in the United States,* Maxine Schwartz Seller, ed. (Westport, CT: Greenwood, 1994), 70–78; and "Nannie Helen Burroughs Papers," *Quarterly Journal of the Library of Congress,* 34 (October 1977), 356–60.

6. Harrison, *The Dream,* 9.

7. Synnott, "Nannie Helen Burroughs" and Easter, *Nannie Helen Burroughs.*

8. Evelyn Brooks Higginbotham, "Nannie Helen Burroughs," in *Black Women in America: An Historical Encyclopedia,* Darlene Clark Hine, Elsa Brown and Rosalyn Terborg-Penn, eds. (Bloomington: Indiana University Press, 1994), 201–05.

9. Easter, *Nannie Helen Burroughs,* 27–34. See also Ethel M. Gordon, *Unfinished Business* (Detroit: Woman's Convention Auxiliary to the National Baptist Convention, 1976) and Sadie Iola Daniel, *Women Builders* (Washington, DC: Associated Publishers, 1970).

10. Nannie Helen Burroughs, "Corresponding Secretary Report for the Executive Committee: Minutes, 1904," 346, in Nannie Helen Burroughs Papers, Library of Congress, Washington, DC (hereafter cited as Burroughs Papers). Other names mentioned for the proposed school included "Woman's Missionary Training School" and "Baptist Training School."

11. Ibid.

12. "First Letter of the Corresponding Secretary," 1901, quoted in Easter, *Nannie Helen Burroughs,* 30.

13. Easter, *Nannie Helen Burroughs,* 58.

14. Harrison, *The Dream,* 10.

15. Woman's Convention, Auxiliary to the National Baptist Convention, "Seventy Five Thousand Dollar Training School for Women and Girls to be Built," promotional flyer, 1908, in Burroughs Papers.

16. National Training School for Women and Girls, "Only One North of Richmond," promotional flyer, 1926, in Burroughs Papers.

17. Easter, *Nannie Helen Burroughs,* 60–63; and National Training School for Women and Girls, "Only One North of Richmond," promotional flyer, 1926, in Burroughs Papers.

18. Daniel, *Women Builders,* 125–29; Synott, "Nannie Helen Burroughs," 72; and National Trade and Professional School, 1951 catalog, Burroughs Papers.

19. Proceedings, Annual Session of the Woman's Convention, Auxiliary of the National Baptist Convention, 1915, Burroughs Papers; Synott, "Nannie Helen Burroughs," 72–73; and National Training School for Women and Girls, "Negroes Who Have Helped Themselves," fund raising brochure, 1930, Burroughs Papers.

20. Easter, *Nannie Helen Burroughs*, 68–70; and Nannie Helen Burroughs, Memorandum for the Trustees of the National Training School for Women and Girls, June 5, 1933, typscript, Burroughs Papers.

21. Carter G. Woodson, "Nannie Burrough's School Fills a Real Need," *The Afro American*, Baltimore, MD, 14 May, 1938, 1.

22. Nannie Helen Burroughs, "The Auditor's Report: Miss Burroughs Defends Her Administration," letter to the editor, *The Washington Bee*, 30 September, 1916, 4.

23. L. K. Williams and R. B. Hudson. Letter to Nannie Helen Burroughs, 29 January 1924, in Burroughs Papers; and Easter, *Nannie Helen Burroughs*, 78–82.

24. Nannie Helen Burroughs, "Statement made by Miss Burroughs at the close of the Annual Report to Woman's Convention, at St. Louis, September 8, 1938," typescript, 2, in Burroughs Papers.

25. "Baptist Convention Hardly Will Re-Open Training School," *The St. Louis Argus*, 5 August 1938, 9.

26. Easter, *Nannie Helen Burroughs*, 118.

27. Nannie Helen Burroughs, *Think on These Things* (Washington, DC: Nannie Helen Burroughs, n.d.).

28. Harrison, *The Dream*, 10.

29. See Holt, *Mary McLeod Bethune*, and McCluskey and Smith (eds.), *Mary McLeod Bethune*. Information about Bethune's childhood largely is derived from an interview with Mary McLeod Bethune by Charles S. Johnson, 1939, Daytona Beach, FL (hereafter cited as Johnson-Bethune interview), microfilm typescript in Mary McLeod Bethune Papers: The Bethune-Cookman College Collection, 1922–1955, Bethune-Cookman College Archives (hereafter cited as Bethune Papers).

30. Johnson-Bethune interview, 3.

31. Ibid., 5.

32. Quoted from a typescript by Frances Keyser, dated 1947, in Bethune Papers.

33. Quoted in Elaine M. Smith, "Mary McLeod Bethune and the National Youth Administration," in *Clio Was a Woman: Studies in the History of American Women*, Mabel E. Deutrich and Virginia C. Purdy, eds. (Washington, DC: Howard University Press, 1980), 149.

34. Quoted in McCluskey and Smith (eds.), *Mary McLeod Bethune*, 85.

35. Mary McLeod Bethune, "Biographical Sketch," typescript, n.d., in Bethune Papers; Audrey Thomas McCluskey, "Introduction," in *Mary McLeod Bethune: Building a Better World, Es-*

says and Selected Documents, Audrey T. McCluskey and Elaine M. Smith, eds., (Bloomington: Indiana University Press, 1999), 3–19; Elaine M. Smith, "Mary McLeod Bethune," in *Notable Black American Women,* Jessie Carney Smith, ed. (Detroit, MI: Gale Research, 1992), 86–92.

36. Information on Lucy Craft Laney is from Jane Bernard-Powers, "Lucy Craft Laney," in *Women Educators in the United States,* Maxine Schwartz Seller, ed. (Westport, CT: Greenwood, 1994), 276–82; Augustus C. Griggs, "Lucy Craft Laney," *Journal of Negro History,* 19, 1934, 97–102; and Casper LeRoy Jordan, "Lucy Laney" in *Notable Black American Women,* Jessie Carney Smith, ed. (Detroit, MI: Gale Research Inc., 1992), 650–52.

37. Johnson, Bethune interview, 33.

38. W.E.B. DuBois, quoted in Beverly Guy-Sheftall, *Daughters of Sorrow, Attitudes Toward Black Women, 1880–1920* (Brooklyn, NY: Carolson, 1990), 35.

39. Mary McLeod Bethune, Sixth Annual Catalogue of the Daytona Educational and Industrial Training School for Negro Girls, reprinted in McCluskey and Smith (eds.), *Mary McLeod Bethune,* 77–78.

40. Mary McLeod Bethune, "What Is the Place of Religion in Higher Education?" unpublished draft for newspaper column, n.d., typescript in Bethune Papers.

41. Holt, *Mary McLeod Bethune,* 128–131.

42. Ibid, 70–92; Genevieve F. Herrick, "Queen Mary: Champion of Negro Women," *Negro History Digest*, December, 1950, 32–39; and Mary McLeod Bethune, quoted in Holt, *Mary McLeod Bethune*, 88.

43. Mary McLeod Bethune, "A Direct Personal Appeal to the Men, Women and Children of My Race," fund raising flyer, 1924, in Bethune Papers; and McCluskey and Smith, *Mary McLeod Bethune*, 68. Elaine Smith, "Introduction to the Mary McLeod Bethune Papers: The Bethune-Cookman College Collection, 1922–55," in *Black Studies Research Sources: Guide to the Microfilm Edition*, John H. Bracey and August Meier, eds. (Bethesda, MD: University, 1995).

44. Ibid.

45. Sheila Y. Flemming, *Bethune-Cookman College*, 1904–1994 (Daytona: Donning Co., 1995), 54–57.

46. Mary McLeod Bethune to Harry Wright McPherson, 26 November 1938, Bethune Papers.

47. Flemming, *Bethune-Cookman College*, 1904–1994, 27–29.

48. Elaine M. Smith, "Womanist Activism: Introduction," in *Mary McLeod Bethune*, McCluskey and Smithe, eds., 131–38.

49. Quoted in "Minutes of the Organizational Meeting of the National Council of Negro Women, 1935," reprinted in *Mary McLeod Bethune*, McCluskey and Smith, eds., 171.

50. Ibid., 172–73; Smith, "Mary McLeod Bethune," in *Notable Black American Women*, Smith, ed., 89.

51. Holt, *Mary McLeod Bethune,* 75.

52. McCluskey, "Introduction," in *Mary McLeod Bethune,* McCluskey and Smith, eds., 15.

53. Eric Anderson and Alfred A. Moss, Jr., *Dangerous Donations: Northern Philanthropy and Southern Black Education, 1902–1930* (Columbia, MO: University of Missouri Press, 1999), 4. Ibid., 36.

54. For discussions of African American educational aims after the Civil War, see Anderson and Moss, *Dangerous Donations;* James D. Anderson, *The Education of Blacks in the South*: 1860–1935 (Chapel Hill: University of North Carolina Press, 1988); and Ronald E. Butchart, *Northern Schools, Southern Blacks, and Reconstruction: Freedmen's Education, 1862-1875* (Westport, CT: Greenwood, 1980).

55. The major biographical sources for this account of the life of Elizabeth Evelyn Wright are J.F.B. Coleman, *Tuskegee to Voorhees,* (Columbia,SC: R.L. Bryan Co., 1922) and J. Kenneth Morris, *Elizabeth Evelyn Wright, Founder of Voorhees College* (Sewanee, TN: University of the South Press, 1983). Primary materials are collected in four voumes compiled by J. Kenneth Morris as "Source Material on the Life of Elizabeth Evelyn Wright,"South Caroliniana Library, University of South Carolina, Columbia, SC (hereafter cited as Wright Collection).

56. *Voorhees Vista,* 6:2 (13 April, 1972), Voorhees College Library.

57. Quoted in Louis R. Harlan, ed., *The Booker T. Washington Papers* (Urbana: University of Illinois Press, 1972), 1:53.

58. Quoted in Coleman, *Tuskegee to Voorhees,* 25.

59. Coleman, *Tuskegee to Voorhees* and Morris, *Elizabeth Evelyn Wright.*

60. Quoted in Coleman, *Tuskegee to Voorhees,* 26. Twenty-ninth Annual Report of the Superintendent of Education of the State of South Carolina (Columbia: State of South Carolina, 1897), 14-15.

61. Coleman, *Tuskegee to Voorhees* and Morris, *Elizabeth Evelyn Wright.*

62. Elizabeth Evelyn Wright to Booker T. Washington, n.d. May, 1906, Wright Collection.

63. Coleman, *Tuskegee to Voorhees* and Morris, *Elizabeth Evelyn Wright.*

64. Elizabeth Evelyn Wright to George Foster Peabody, 21 December, 1901, Wright Collection.

65. Martha Schofield to Emily Howland, 6 March, 1901, Wright Collection.

66. Morris, *Elizabeth Evelyn Wright,* 150-51.

67. Elizabeth Evelyn Wright to Booker T. Washington, 18 February, 1904. Quoted in Morris, *Elizabeth Evelyn Wright,* 196.

68. *Bamberg (SC) Herald,* 20 December 1906, 2.

Chapter Five

1. Kate Rousmaniere, *City Teachers: Teaching and School Reform in Historical Perspective.* (New York: Teachers College Press, 1997), 94.

2. Ibid., 28.

3. Willie Nelms, *Cora Wilson Stewart: Crusader Against Illiteracy* (Jefferson, NC: McFarland & Company, 1997), 3.

4. The first significant treatment of Cora Wilson Stewart was Florence Estes's unpublished 1988 doctoral dissertation, *Cora Wilson Stewart and the Moonlight Schools of Kentucky, 1911–1920.* From a historical outlook, Estes describes educational movements that influenced Stewart's work in Kentucky and provides some useful perspectives on certain aspects of Stewart's life. However, Willie Nelms's full-scale biography, *Cora Wilson Stewart: Crusader Against Illiteracy* and William A. Link's book, *The Paradox of Southern Progressivism, 1880–1930,* were the most useful sources in the preparation of Stewart's biographical data for this chapter. Wherever possible, Stewart's own words from her 1922 book, *Moonlight Schools: For the Emancipation of Adult Illiterates,* are placed in the context of educational philosophies.

5. Florence Estes, *Cora Wilson Stewart and the Moonlight Schools of Kentucky,* 1911–1920 (Ed.D. Dissertation, University of Kentucky, 1988), 67.

6. Ibid., 77.

7. Ibid., 80.

8. Ibid., 67.

9. Ibid., 77.

10. Ibid., 80.

11. Nelms, *Cora Wilson Stewart,* 24.

12. Ibid., 22.

13. Ibid., 31.

14. Estes, *Cora Wilson Stewart,* 54.

15. Nelms, *Cora Wilson Stewart,* 32–33.

16. Kentucky Illiteracy Commission, First Biennial Report, 1914–1915 (Louisville, 1916), 2–9.

17. Cora Wilson Stewart, Moonlight Schools for the Emancipation of Adult Illiterates (New York: Duttton , 1922), 9.

18. Nelms, *Cora Wilson Stewart,* 35.

19. William A. Link, *The Paradox of Southern Progressivism, 1880–1930* (Chapel Hill, NC: The University of North Carolina Press, 1992), 139.

20. Kentucky Illiteracy Commission, First Biennial Report, 2–9.

21. Link, The Paradox of Southern Progressivism, 140.

22. Stewart, Moonlight Schools, 18.

23. Nelms, Cora Wilson Stewart, 38.

24. Ibid., 41.

25. Kentucky Illiteracy Commission, First Biennial Report, 2–9.

26. Stewart, *Moonlight Schools*, 18.

27. Nelms, *Cora Wilson Stewart*, 41.

28. Link, *The Paradox of Southern Progressivism*, 140.

29. Stewart, *Moonlight Schools*, 89.

30. Ibid., 2–9.

31. Stewart, *Moonlight Schools*, 19.

32. Ibid., 68.

33. Ibid., 82.

34. Ibid., 48.

35. Link, *The Paradox of Southern Prog*ressivism, 141.

36. Ibid., 141.

37. Ibid., 142.

38. Stewart, *Moonlight Schools*, 5.

39. Nelms, *Cora Wilson Stewart,* 78.

40. Stewart, *Moonlight Schools,* 159.

41. Ibid., 159.

42. Ibid., 159.

43. Ibid., 56.

44. Ibid., 145.

45. Stewart, *Moonlight Schools,* 28.

46. Ibid., 154.

47. Ibid., 3.

48. Stewart, *Moonlight Schools,* 1–2.

49. Ibid., 5.

50. Ibid. 5.

51. Nelms, *Cora Wilson Stewart,* 72–73.

52. David L. Carlton, *Mill and Town in South Carolina 1880–1920* (Baton Rouge, LA: Louisiana State University Press, 1982), 7.

53. Ibid., 11.

54. Wil Lou Gray, *A Night School Experiment in Laurens County* (Columbia: State Department of Education, 1915).

55. See "Our Paper," a four-page list of simple sentences for copying, used in Newberry County sometime between 1914 and 1917 (Wil Lou Gray Papers, SCL).

56. DaMaris E. Ayres, *Let My People Learn: The Biography of Dr. Wil Lou Gray* (Greenwood, SC: Attic, 1988), 1.

57. Harvey G. Neufeldt, "South Carolina's Wil Lou Gray: A Study in Education and Gender" (*Vitae Scholasticae*, Fall 1979, Volume 16, Number 2), 52.

58. Neufeldt, *Vitae Scholasticae*, 53; Montgomery, *South Carolina's Wil Lou Gray*, 2.

59. Audio tape interview of Dr. Wil Lou Gray conducted in June, 1974. Special Collections of the South Caroliniana Library, Columbia, South Carolina.

60. Audio tape interview of Dr. Wil Lou Gray conducted in June 1974. Special Collections of the South Caroliniana Library, Columbia, South Carolina.

61. South Carolina Educational Television [SC ETV] Network Production, Interview: Wil Lou Gray, 1973.

62. Audio tape interview of Dr. Wil Lou Gray conducted in June 1974. Special Collections of the South Caroliniana Library, Columbia, South Carolina.

63. Audio tape interview of Dr. Wil Lou Gray conducted in June, 1974. Special Collections of the South Caroliniana Library, Columbia, South Carolina.

64. Neufeldt, *Vitae Scholasticae,* 52.

65. Ibid., 53.

66. Ibid., 53.

67. Montgomery, *South Carolina's Wil Lou Gray,* 78.

68. Ayres, *Let My People,* 75; South Carolina Educational Television interview of Wil Lou Gray, February 11, 1975. Museum of Education at the University of South Carolina Archives.

69. Ayres, *Let My People,* 75.

70. SC ETV interview of Wil Lou Gray, February 11, 1975

71. Henry Lesesne, "Better-Late-Than-Never Students: South Carolina's Opportunity School" (*The Christian Science Monitor,* Saturday August 5, 1961) p. 4.

72. South Carolina Educational Television Network, Wil Lou Gray TV interview, 1973.

73. Neufeldt, *Vitae Scholasticae,* 53.

74. Carlton, *Mill and Town,* 263.

75. Mabel Montgomery, South Carolina's Wil Lou Gray: Pioneer in Adult Education, A Crusader, Modern Model (Columbia, SC, The Opportunity School, 1963).

76. Carlton, *Mill and Town,* 264.

77. Ibid., 264.

78. South Carolina Educational Television Network, Wil Lou Gray TV interview, 1973.

79. South Carolina Educational Television Network, Wil Lou Gray TV interview, 1973.

80. Erin Kohn, Editor-in-Chief, *The Open Door* (Due West, S.C.: The Opportunity Schools, 1929), 17.

81. Neufeldt, *Vitae Scholasticae,* 59.

82. South Carolina Educational Television Network, Wil Lou Gray interview, 1973.

83. Ayres, *Let My People Learn,* 114–116; Montgomery, *South Carolina's Wil Lou Gray,* 4–43; Norfleet Hardy, *Farm, Mill, and Classroom: A History of Tax Supported Adult Education in South Carolina to 1960* (Columbia, SC: The University of South Carolina, 1967), 82–84. Neufeldt, *Vitae Scholasticae,* 59. (DAR was part of Gray's network; she herself, was a member.)

84. Montgomery, *South Carolina's Wil Lou Gray,* 43.

85. Ibid., 47.

86. Kohn, *The Open Door,* 18.

87. *Florence Morning News,* (Florence, S.C. Tuesday, October 24, 1950)

88. Montgomery, *South Carolina's Wil Lou Gray,* 43.

89. Kohn, *The Open Door,* 18.

90. Kohn, *The Open Door,* 23.

91. Ibid., 30-31.

92. Montgomery, *South Carolina's Wil Lou Gray,* 49.

93. Ayres, *Let My People Learn,* 160.

94. Ibid., 161.

95. Sixty-eighth Annual Report of Superintendent of Education (Columbia: State Department of Education, 1936), 65.

96. Seventieth Annual Report of Superintendent of Education (Columbia: State Department of Education, 1938), 72.

97. Neufeldt, *Vitae Scholasticae,* 51.

98. Ibid., 54.

99. Stewart, Moonlight Schools, ix.

100. Debbie Mauldin Cottrell, *Pioneer Woman Educator: The Progressive Spirit of Annie Webb Blanton* (College Station, TX: Texas A&M University Press, 1993).

101. Debbie Mauldin Cottrell, "Professional, Feminine, and Feminist: Annie Webb Blanton and the Founding of Delta Kappa Gamma" in *Women and Texas History: Selected Essays* ,Fane Downs and Nancy Baker Jones, eds. (Austin, TX: State Historical Association), 88–101.

102. Cottrell, *Pioneer Woman,* 108.

103. Anne Firor Scott, *Southern Lady: From Pedestal to Politics, 1830–1930* (Chicago: University of Chicago Press, 1970), 163.

104. Anne Firor Scott, *Natural Allies* (Urbana, IL: University of Illinois Press, 1993), 2.

105. *Dallas Morning News,* July 28, 30, 1918.

106. Debbie Mauldin Cottrell, *Annie Webb Blanton, 1870-1945,* http://www.utexas.edu/courses/mis311/history, paragraph 3.

107. Ibid., paragraph 4.

108. Cottrell, "Professional, Feminine, and Feminist," 91.

109. Eunah Temple Holden, *Our Heritage in the Delta Kappa Gamma Societ,* Vol. *1* (Austin, TX: Delta Kappa Gamma Society, 1960), 7.

110. Ibid.

111. Ibid., xx.

112. Ibid., 7.

113. Cottrell, *Annie Webb Blanton, 1870-1945,* paragraph 5.

114. Ibid.

115. Cottrell, *Pioneer Woman,* 162.

116. Nancy F. Cott, *The Grounding of Modern Feminism* (New Haven: Yale University Press, 1987), 89, 90, 92, 230.

117. Cott, *The Grounding,* 90, 92.

118. Clara M. Parker, *Annie Webb Blanton, Founder: The Delta Kappa Gamma Society* (Austin: Delta Kappa Gamma Society, 1949), 33–34.

119. Cottrell, *Pioneer Woman,* 111.

120. Ibid., 112

121. Fane Downs and Nancy Baker Jones (Eds.), *Women and Texas History: Selected Essays* (Austin: Texas State Historical Association, 1993) , xi–xviii.

122. Debbie Mauldin Cottrell, *Annie Webb Blanton,* paragraph 6.

Chapter Six

1. Margaret Smith Crocco, Petra Munro, and Kathleen Weiler,

2. *Pedagogies of Resistance: Women Educator Activists, 1880–1960* (New York: Teachers College Press, 1999), 1.

3. Amy Thompson McCandless, *The Past in the Present: Women's Higher Education in the Twentieth Century American South* (Tuscaloosa: The University of Alabama Press, 1999), 21.

4. Joseph F. Kett, "Women and the Progressive Impulse in Southern Education," in *The Web of Southern Social Relations:*

Women, Family, and Education, Walter J. Fraser, Jr., R. Frank Saunders, Jr., and Jon L. Wakelyn, eds. (Athens, GA: The University of Georgia Press, 1985), 166–80.

5. Robyn Muncy, *Creating a Female Dominion in American Reform, 1890–1935* (New York: Oxford University Press, 1991), xii–xiii.

6. Ellison Durant Smith, Congressional Record, 74th Congress, 1st Session, 5749.

7. Crocco et al., Pedagogies of Resistance, 116.

8. Penina Migdal Glazer and Miriam Slater, *Unequal Colleagues: The Entrance of Women into the Professions, 1890–1940* (New Brunswick: Rutgers University Press, 1987), 211–12.

9. Ibid., 217.

Index

HISTORY OF SCHOOLS & SCHOOLING

THIS SERIES EXPLORES THE HISTORY OF SCHOOLS AND SCHOOLING in the United States and other countries. Books in this series examine the historical development of schools and educational processes, with special emphasis on issues of educational policy, curriculum and pedagogy, as well as issues relating to race, class, gender, and ethnicity. Special emphasis will be placed on the lessons to be learned from the past for contemporary educational reform and policy. Although the series will publish books related to education in the broadest societal and cultural context, it especially seeks books on the history of specific schools and on the lives of educational leaders and school founders.

For additional information about this series or for the submission of manuscripts, please contact the general editors:

Alan R. Sadovnik
Rutgers University-Newark
Education Dept.
155 Conklin Hall
175 University Avenue
Newark, NJ 07102

Susan F. Semel
The City College of New York, CUNY
138th Street and Convent Avenue
NAC 5/208
New York, NY 10031

To order other books in this series, please contact our Customer Service Department:

800-770-LANG (within the U.S.)
212-647-7706 (outside the U.S.)
212-647-7707 FAX

Or browse online by series at:

www.peterlangusa.com